OURSELVES
Why We Are Who We Are

A Handbook for Educators

BOOKS BY FRANK SMITH

Ourselves: Why We Are Who We Are

Understanding Reading (six editions)

Writing and the Writer (two editions)

Reading Without Nonsense (four editions)
(*Reading* in UK)

Insult to Intelligence

to think

Whose Language? What Power?

The Book of Learning and Forgetting

The Glass Wall: Why Mathematics Can Seem Difficult

Edited Volumes

The Genesis of Language (with George Miller)

Psycholinguistics and Reading

Awakening to Literacy (with Hillel Goelman
and Antoinette A. Oberg)

Essays

Essays Into Literacy

Joining the Literacy Club

Between Hope and Havoc

Unspeakable Acts, Unnatural Practices

OURSELVES
Why We Are Who We Are

A Handbook for Educators

Frank Smith

LAWRENCE ERLBAUM ASSOCIATES, PUBLISHERS
2006   Mahwah, New Jersey   London

Lawrence Erlbaum Associates, Inc., Publishers
10 Industrial Avenue
Mahwah, New Jersey 07430
www.erlbaum.com

Cover design by Kathryn Houghtaling Lacey

Library of Congress Cataloging-in-Publication Data

Smith, Frank, 1928–   .
    Ourselves : why we are who we are : a handbook for educators / Frank Smith.
        p. cm.
    Includes bibliographical references and index.
ISBN 0-8058-5954-3 (cloth : alk. paper)
ISBN 0-8058-5955-1 (pbk. : alk. paper)
1. Reflective teaching. 2. Learning, Psychology of. 3. Self. 4. Self-actualization (Psychology). 5. Knowledge, Theory of. 6. Education—Philosophy. I. Title: Why we are who we are : a handbook for educators.   II. Title.
LB1025.3.S63   2006
371.102—dc22   2005054411
                                                              CIP

Books published by Lawrence Erlbaum Associates are printed on acid-free paper, and their bindings are chosen for strength and durability.

Printed in the United States of America
10   9   8   7   6   5   4   3   2   1

Contents

Preface

What a piece of work is a man, mused Hamlet, how noble in reason, how infinite in faculty. He was including women, of course. This book is a reflective study of that piece of work.

I'm particularly concerned with how we become *Ourselves*—with why we are who we are. Unlike Hamlet, I don't especially credit us with a noble faculty of reason. There's no doubt that we are smart, but we also have limitations and can be guilty of stupidities. Human beings are compassionate and loving, no doubt about that either. But we can also be callous, cruel, and murderous.

怆́

This book delves into how we come to terms with ourselves, with other people, and with the world in general. It is about how we come to be what we are and to think the way we do. It is a book about *influences*.

One enormous influence on everyone is the other people we grow up with, starting from birth and continuing as we grow, as we develop, throughout the span of our life. Another great influence is obviously the circumstances in which we find ourselves, including our geographic location, health, wealth, and social status. Another is the manner in which we are educated, including the television we watch, the books we read, the music we hear, and the movies and other visual experiences that are part of our lives. And finally, there is the company we keep.

Most of these influences are a consequence of chance. Different circumstances could have made us different people. Some of these circumstances we could change. But some influences are permanent fixtures in our lives. They change us, and as individuals we have no way of changing them, no matter what we do.

A particular influence that is a central consideration of this book is *language*, not just in terms of the communicative networks that it engages us in—the "information" that presents itself to us—but in the largely unsuspected framework for thought that lies within language itself. It is through the conceptual aspects of language that much of what we think and perceive appears to be self-evident to us. Language can inspire us to the noblest of sentiments, but it can also make us instruments of ideologies. We may think of language as a neutral factor in our lives, a tool that we use to accomplish ends. We don't suspect that language could be different and that, if it were, we would think differently.

Finally, I consider the role of *technology*. People have always seen the world as self-evident, including its technology, even when there has been precious little technology in that world. But perceptions change with technology. Current technology looks up-to-date, and former technology looks dated. People don't change—our minds haven't evolved for the past 10,000 years at least. But technology has changed at an ever-increasing rate, and so—at an ever-increasing rate—is the close relationship that people have with technology. We accept our technology; it is the way the world has to be. We even take the credit for making technology what it is today—as if any of us has a significant say in how technology has evolved.

It is impossible to think of people today—of their personal, social, cultural, economic, ethical, and intellectual lives—without thinking of language and technology. What is obvious about the world we live in today, including the way we think and behave, is what language and technology tell us is obvious.

Something I don't discuss in this book is the inner workings of the human brain. I write about what can be observed, not philosophized about. The things I am interested in—thinking, learning, understanding, remembering—have never been found in the brain. Researchers don't even know what to look for. They are sure the brain must be responsible for thinking, learning, understanding, and remembering, but they've never had any luck in finding them in the structure of the brain. They've never found any trace in the brain of other things that make us human, like will, intentions, desire, values, even enjoyment. My argument is that these things are aspects of people as a whole, as individuals, but they are not parts of them. Obviously people are able to recall things, but that isn't because they have some kind of memory store inside—or outside—their head. Obviously things go on all the time in the brain—but this doesn't mean that thinking, learning, understanding, and remembering occur in the brain. It explains nothing to say "the brain does it" if these things can't be found in the brain.

We see images on the television screen, but it would be pointless to look inside the system for the images we see on the screen. What goes on behind the screen no doubt makes the images possible, but the screen is the only place where the images occur. (This is not the best of analogies for the human situation—but I don't think there is a perfect one.) A person can be seen to be thinking, learning, understanding, and remembering, and doubtless what goes on in the brain makes these things possible. But thinking, learning, understanding, and remembering are characteristics of people as a whole, not mechanisms to be found inside their head.

My aim in this book is to describe the scope and limits for how we can be seen to think, learn, understand, and remember, but not to "explain" such behavior by recourse to hypothetical inner entities. In other words, this is a book of description not of explanation. These are two quite different intellectual territories. *Describers* are people like novelists and poets, who want to express what they see and feel but rarely speculate about the reason for it all. *Explainers* are usually researchers and scientists who want to find reasons for what they see, and constantly speculate, calling their speculations *hypotheses*.

Of course, all describers hypothesize from time to time—"Why was he late again?"—this is part of human nature. And all explainers describe from time to time—what else would they have to pin their hypotheses to? But explainers usually find their descriptions ready made, they acquire them off-the-peg or from language. Describers think about what they are describing.

To repeat, this is a book of descriptions, not of explanations.

ॐ

In particular, this is a book of relevance to educators. Teachers and others with classroom responsibilities are constantly barraged with instructions and suggestions from others further up the educational hierarchy or outside it, whose actual experience of working with students is distant or nonexistent. Many directives are based on what is called *brain research*, supposedly at the cutting edge of science but actually far removed from the front lines of education.

Solemn pronouncements are usually made by educators with little understanding of neurology and by neuroscientists with little understanding of education.

Teachers know their own students best—or they should—and no outsider is qualified to prescribe the course of action to be taken for any particular student at any particular time. Learning and teaching are part of a social collaboration that can never be scripted in advance.

Ourselves outlines the possibilities and limitations inherent in all of us. It delineates who we are. But it also stresses that no two of us are the same, or that what we become depends on the experiences we have on our journey in life and the people we encounter on the way. The formal part of learning that is called *education* is particularly sensitive to the role of people who organize critical experiences for us, who are our *teachers*.

At the end of each chapter is a brief summary. I try especially in these summaries to reinforce and highlight points that are of particular relevance to teachers.

ACKNOWLEDGMENT

"Where do you get your ideas from?" I am sometimes asked. The comment is made because I rarely name anyone who might have been the source of things I write. Recently someone said, "Who are you for, and who are you against? Why don't you tell us who these people are?"

My response is that I usually don't write about people, for them or against them. I write about ideas. And I don't see ideas as belonging to any particular person—especially not to me. I don't see ideas as the kind of things individuals possess or make. I'm perfectly happy to admit that there may not be a single idea in this book that was original with me (though I would claim originality for the way all the ideas in the book are put together; this is not a work of plagiarism).

I see ideas in much the way that I see technology (chap. 10), not so much devised by one particular person (not even the "inventor") as by generations of predecessors. And the transmission is not from one person to another, but from technology at one stage of its evolution to technology at another stage, with individuals as the intermediaries. Newton said he saw further by standing on the shoulders of giants. Every inventor stands on, and adds to, technology that has already evolved. And every idea arises from ideas that have existed in the past.

I have no way of cataloging where the ideas in this book came from. I happily credit everyone who has been part of the experience that expresses itself in this book—the authors of the books and articles I have read, the presenters of the lectures I have heard, and the many people I have had conversations with, formally or informally. I give credit whether I have "agreed" with these people or not (usually, it is a bit of each). What has mattered is that in these exchanges, ideas have flourished. Getting ideas, like every other aspect of thinking, is an active, selective, and constructive process.

About the Author

Frank Smith

Frank Smith is a writer and researcher living on Vancouver Island, British Columbia, Canada. He was born in England, took his undergraduate degree at the University of Western Australia, and has a PhD in psycholinguistics from Harvard University.

As a reporter and editor, he was on the staff of a number of newspapers and magazines in Europe and Australia. As a researcher, he has been associated with many projects concerned with literacy and language education. He was a professor at the Ontario Institute for Studies in Education and the Linguistics Department of the University of Toronto for 12 years, and subsequently was Lansdowne Professor of Language in Education at the University of Victoria, British Columbia,

Canada. In 1992, he was distinguished visiting professor and head of a new Department of Applied English Language Studies at the University of the Witwatersrand in Johannesburg, South Africa.

Frank Smith has published short stories, poetry, a novel, and over 20 books concerned with language and education. They include six editions of *Understanding Reading* and two editions of *Writing and the Writer*, published by Lawrence Erlbaum Associates; *Insult to Intelligence, Essays Into Literacy, Joining the Literacy Club, Between Hope and Havoc*, and *Unspeakable Acts, Unnatural Practices*, published by Heinemann Educational Books; and *Reading Without Nonsense* (four editions), *to think, The Glass Wall* (mathematics), and *The Book of Learning and Forgetting*, published by Teachers College Press.

He also coedited *Awakening to Literacy* (Heinemann Educational Books) on the growth of children's awareness of written language, and compiled *Whose Language? What Power?* (Teachers College Press) on the politics of second language teaching in South Africa.

His current research interests focus on psychological, social, and cultural consequences of human technology, including language.

1

Our Myths

A number of common words have given headaches to philosophers for a couple of thousand years and to scientific researchers for about 150 years. These are words like:

thinking, learning, remembering, and *understanding*
(or *comprehension*).

The philosophical and scientific problems would never arise if we regarded the words simply as descriptions of people, seen from the outside. We can observe these aspects of people without having to look inside them in any way. You know perfectly well what I mean when I say my friend Fred is thinking, learning, remembering, or understanding something. You don't have to imagine some mechanisms inside Fred doing those things for him. That is the way I use the words in this book, simply as descriptions of observable states of affairs.

I won't be using these words to refer to some mysterious place, process, or state inside Fred's body. But here's where many people get confused. Language encourages us to believe that thinking, learning, remembering, and understanding are done by particular mechanisms *inside* the body, usually in the brain. We can *remember*, for example, because memories are stored somewhere. Language does this for us. It establishes myths. We have words for things that don't actually exist, that are myths—words like *ether, griffon, unicorn,* and *mermaid,* for example.

Perfectly good *descriptive* words like those on my list are believed to refer to some part or process *within* the brain. Scientists look for locations for thinking, learning, remembering, and understanding but can never find them. They are as elusive as the end of the rainbow.

Nevertheless, scientists think mechanisms for thinking, learning, remembering, and understanding must exist somewhere in the body. They think this because (1) they tend to believe that there must be something inside the body to account for everything that can be seen from the outside, and (2) language encourages them to have these ideas.

The significant question, I believe, is not what there is in the body to support these descriptive terms, but rather how these descriptive terms got into language in the first place. The word *believe*, which I have just employed, is a case in point. I'm sure you weren't confused when I used the word. It told you something about me. But there would have been confusion if you thought there was some inner part of me that was doing the believing. You might say, because of something you have heard or read, that my brain is doing my believing for me. But does that way of thinking increase your understanding, or make you more scientific? If my brain is doing my believing for me, what am *I* doing? This is the kind of stuff that philosophical mystery is made of.

The inquiry we are embarking upon is neither philosophical nor physiological. It doesn't ask abstruse (and unnecessary) questions like "What is thinking?" or "Where is thinking?" The inquiry is linguistic. It asks how such confusing words got into language in the first place. We'll look at the way people talk, not at diagrams of the brain.

WHERE IS MEMORY?

Let's take memory as an example. It's a good place to start because it takes the bull by the horns. Many people, I find, are convinced that they have memories stored away somewhere in their brains. No doubt you believe that too. It's not easy for me to make the case that though you certainly can remember numerous things from your past, you don't do this by retrieving memories from some inner store.

I have difficulty starting this discussion with many people because they say, "Of course memory exists. I can remember innumerable things about my childhood"—which they proceed to demonstrate at great length. And when I say that I'm not trying to deny them the ability to remember, only that I don't think this is because they have a memory store in their brain, they say, "So where is memory, then? It has to be somewhere. Is it inside the body or outside?" And when I respond that my question is not whether memory is inside or outside, but whether a store called *memory* exists at all, they say, "Of course memory exists. I've got one"—and proceed with another lengthy list of childhood recollections.

I plan to approach the matter in two ways. First, I'll explain why the existence of a store of specific memories in a particular place in the body is highly dubious, despite all the efforts of scientists to find it. Second, I'll explain how we are able to recall countless things without having a special store of memories.

But I should explain why this matter is important to me right now and why I am compelled to engage in all this semantic nit-picking before getting on with the main parts of the book. The book is about people, it is about *ourselves*, and my intention is to be both logical and scientific. But I can't be logical or scientific if I fill my chapters with allusions to mysterious, mythical, and undetectable faculties inside the human body. That's as bad as phrenology. I only want to talk about what can be seen, understood, and discussed, without recourse to abstruse theory or unassailable mysticism.

THE DOUBTFUL STATUS OF MEMORY

We never say, "I have such happy memories of last summer in my brain"; we simply say we have happy memories, referring to all not part of us. And we don't *feel* that we have memories in our brain; we feel that memory is somehow attached to us as a whole. In fact, the only reason we might bring the brain into the discussion at all is because someone at some time has told us (or written) that the brain is the location of our memories. We'd never have guessed otherwise. I don't feel that something in my head is involved when I remember something. I couldn't tell you any specific part of me where I feel that memory is located. I just have to say, "In all of me." I would say, "It's *my* memory, not my brain's." The memory is in all of me, not a part.

Despite all the efforts of psychologists and neurologists, no one has been able to find a location for memory in the brain. Back in 1950, the renowned brain researcher Karl Lashley wrote an article entitled "In Search of the Engram"—*engram* being a technical word for a memory trace in the brain. He reported that, despite years of searching, he had been unable to find any trace of what might be called a memory system or a memory store in the human brain. His conclusion was that memory must be distributed throughout the brain. The entire brain was a memory-creating and storage system. But he still kept looking for some specific sign of "memory," as have thousands of researchers ever since. But there has been no success.

There are other clues that memory is not something that will be easily found inside the human body. Psychologists can't even agree on what memory is—they don't really know what they're looking for. Some psychologists divide memory into a couple of processes—a short-term memory, which is quickly formed but quickly lost—and a long-term memory, which is basically part of everything we know. But what these psychologists call short-term memory, others would say is simply attention. It is what we happen to be doing right now. Long-term memory, on the other hand, is everything we know; it might just as well be called knowledge. So by a simple sleight of hand, memory has been made to disappear, to be replaced by attention and knowledge.

Other psychologists, to complicate matters, agree there are two kinds of memory but characterize them in different ways. They distinguish, for example, *episodic* memory—for what is going on at the moment—from *semantic* memory—or the way memories are stored. But this obviously applies only to memories that can be put into words. What about visual memories, or auditory memories? We remember scenes, we remember voices, and we can remember anything else we can perceive, like tastes, odors, and tactile sensations. How can all these be part of a general phenomenon we call memory?

Memory is a record in the present of things that happened in the past, just as all the dents and scratches on the side of my car are a record of the experiences it has had in the past. We're able to describe events in our past experience, but it is notoriously difficult to put them in correct order. Memory isn't a tape that runs over time, or a push down storage device, such as a computer has.

Which reminds me—it is quite inappropriate to talk of a computer having a memory or memory devices. Everything that is in a computer is in the present—what memory it has is part of its current state and operations. We use so much metaphorical language to discuss computers in human terms, and humans in computer terms, that I make a point of not discussing computers in this book. Computers aren't human; "ourselves" would not be an appropriate term to refer to both people and computers.

MEMORIES WITHOUT MEMORY

Everyone knows that memory can't be trusted. We "suppress" memories we don't want to think about and embellish memories to suit current purposes. The British psychologist Frederick Bartlett, back in the 1930s, famously demonstrated that what we call memories of past events are actually mental reconstructions colored by cultural attitudes and personal habits. He showed that very little of an event is actually perceived at the time of its occurrence, and that in recalling such events, gaps in observation or perception are filled in with the aid of current knowledge.

I prefer to think that memories are *constructions* rather than reconstructions—they are not so much made from the past as from the present. All our past experience has gone into what we are today, and our memories are constructed from what we are today.

We don't need a special place for memories because everything we can construct of the past is embedded in us at present. It is not in us as a special part; it is what we are made of. You don't need to consult special memories to discover that you had a happy childhood or an adventurous youth; the events of your past have made you who you are today. *Everything in your past is in your present.*

Everything we can "retrieve" from history exists in the present—even old documents or records of old documents. The rings in the trunk of a tree were accumulated in the past but they exist in the present, like the dents in my car and the scars on my body. These are not in a separate part of the tree, my car, or me, where memories are recorded and contained. They are present evidence of what happened in the past, mementoes but not memories.

What has made us what we are right now? Our previous experiences. And where can we locate these previous experiences? Nowhere. They are not *part* of us; they have *become* us.

How is it possible that our experiences have become built into us in such a fundamental and all-enveloping way? Why do they have such lasting consequences that they can be resurrected, or rather constructed? I can explain it all in two words:

We grow.

GROWTH

Humans are not static creatures. We are constantly growing and renewing ourselves.

We don't grow incrementally, by adding bits to ourselves. Instead, elements of everything we are today were with us at birth (or before). We grow like plants and trees, flourishing in every respect, in size, strength, and ability. And growth—development—continues throughout our lives. Growth is not an occasional side effect of special circumstances; it is a constant condition of existence.

The way we grow is a function of our experience. I can't look back into the past for a record of the particular factors that contributed to my growth, but I can look at myself now for evidence of where I have been.

Because we grow, we learn. Learning is the growth of what we know and can do. Every moment we have moved on from where we were before, not just physically, but in terms of knowledge, understanding, and values. We don't need to look into the past to discover what we have learned, or what we can understand or sympathize with. There is no *store* of knowledge, values, and understanding; everything permeates what we are right now.

WORDS FOR PEOPLE, WORDS FOR PARTS

Suppose—to go back to my original point—there is no such thing as memory at all. It's a useful way to talk about ourselves and other people, but it doesn't refer to anything inside us. We've got the word—*memory*—but where did the word come from? Why should anyone have thought there was such a thing as memory in the first place, in order for such a word to be invented? And why should such a word have become established in the language, even though it has caused psychologists, philosophers, and other analytical individuals such anguish and fruitless search? It is because words that are perfectly useful and comprehensible when applied to people, as a whole, become totally misleading if taken to refer to a part of them.

The same applies to many other words referring to attributes of people. We can say that someone is proud, happy, anxious, miserable, or hungry, but not that some part of them is proud, happy, anxious, and so forth. These are all person words; they don't apply to parts. The same applies when we say that we, and other people, have a mind.

These words apply only to the observable entirety of people. We can't say that a part of a person is proud, happy, or anxious, or that it is something *inside* the person that is in those states. It is quite unjustifiable to assert that there is something inside the person, or part of the person, that is proud, happy, or anxious on behalf of the person as a whole. We may have hypotheses about what causes our feelings, but we locate the feelings outside the body, not inside. Even if a particular balance of chemicals in the brain is detected, it still has to be correlated with observation of a person as a whole. Simply looking at an X-ray, an MRI, or a blood sample won't tell you if a person is happy.

There is an unfortunate tendency among scientific researchers— though automobile mechanics know better—to assume that if part of a system is damaged and the entire system breaks down, then the damaged part is where the system is located. People will argue, for example, that memory is contained within the *cingulate gyrus*, deep inside the brain, because if the *gyrus* is damaged by illness or accident, memory may be severely affected. That's like arguing that if your car won't start because the battery is dead, the battery is what drives the car.

As I have said, scientists have never been able to find mechanisms and locations in the brain for thinking, memory, learning, and understanding. But many assume they must be there, and have spent over a century in fruitless pursuit of them. They never think that the way something appears on the outside, as an aspect of a whole person, need not be attributed to a part of that person, outside or inside. They would never expect to find general aspects of a cake—its consistency and moistness, for example—in any of the implements or ingredients that went into the making of the cake.

What has sent scientists on this fruitless pursuit? *Language.* The words exist, therefore scientists, and many others, assume the objects the words refer to must exist. It is time to look at how the words got into language.

THE REFLECTIVE FLIP

There's another reason why I emphasize that person words should not be attributed to parts of people, especially not to the inside of them. And that is because we have no access to what is going on in our own bodies, to supposed mechanisms or stores. Everything we believe about the inside of our bodies, someone else has told us, or we have read.

Where Do Our *Ideas* About Ourselves Come From?

We would never have said that we have a mind, or memory, unless there were words in the language suggesting to us that such things existed. We wouldn't even know we had a brain unless someone had told us so. We don't detect things about ourselves, which we then put names to. We encounter the words and apply those words to something we put inside ourselves and other people.

Everything we know about ourselves we have got from other people, either from what they have told us (or written) or simply by observation of them. The basis of language (and of learning) is social. We see (or read about) other people, and assume that we're like them. I call it *the reflective flip.* We don't learn what we're like from looking inside ourselves, but from looking at other people. And not from looking inside them, but from looking at the outside of them. (We have plenty of technology for looking inside people, but we still have to look at their outside, or ask them, to ascertain what they are doing or feeling.)

Often, of course, we make assumptions about what is going on inside other people. But once again, we can only do this because of language. We can't *see* memory, understanding, or learning inside other people, even with X-rays and other devices. We only have language to tell us that *they* have a mind and memory, just like us. The only reason we agree that other people might have a mind or memory is from what we observe on the outside, from their behavior. Language tells us that there are inner correlates of these things, but we have no way of checking. We have no way of checking on the people who tell us we have things like minds and memories inside ourselves. They can never show us these things.

Where Do Our *Words* About Ourselves Come From?

How do we come to believe we have a mind, a memory, consciousness, that we learn and have a self? How do we know we have kidneys, or a nervous system, or aspirations for the future? We can't look inside ourselves to see any of these things—and the people who first discovered that we had them didn't do so by examining themselves, inside or out.

All of these ideas we have about ourselves came from looking at other people and from the language that we use to talk about other people. The reflective flip again. We look at other people, make assumptions about them, and then reflect those assumptions back on ourselves.

We know we have a brain and a heart—and that we think with the former and not the latter—because of what we have been told or read in books. I'm prepared to accept the general wisdom that I have lungs, kidneys, and a liver, though I have no way of finding this out for myself. (Even X-rays and MRIs would be totally opaque to me, so to speak, without someone telling me what exactly I'm looking at. And how did these experts learn the names and functions of these parts of bodies? By looking at other bodies and reflecting their conclusions back upon themselves.)

The same conditions must have applied for the development of language. Where did words like *honesty, generosity*, or *charm* come from? Not by earlier speakers examining themselves and thinking, "I've got to invent a word for this aspect of me." These proto-speakers observed particular behaviors in other people, found words to summarize those characteristics, and then attributed the characteristics to themselves. They flipped their assumptions about other people inside themselves. They doubtless also characterized other people as dishonest, ungenerous, or uncharming—and declared that these were characteristics that they personally did *not* have.

Words don't come from nowhere. They must have a meaning or a function. And the meaning of people words comes from observation of other people (or of visible objects). The few words that might be thought to have got a meaning directly from ourselves, like *pain* and *emotions*, were not acquired by going on inner journeys. They arose from seeing ourselves from the outside, like another person, observing that we had pain and feelings—provided we understood the appropriate words. (Infants, lacking the specific words, just feel hurt and unhappy when all is not well with them.)

Where Abstract Words Come From

Even abstract terms like *altruism, idealism*, and *chivalry* must have originated as descriptions of the observable behavior of others. Or from language itself, on a basis of words that were simple descriptors of other people's behavior. Thus we might reasonably say that someone has done something *good*, and falsely extrapolate from there that there is something called *goodness*, which the observed person possesses, and which we therefore conclude we can apply to ourselves. From there we might go as far as to say there is an entity called *The Good*, which permeates good deeds and good people—though all we have done is invent a few words.

But we didn't get these ideas by looking at the inside of people, and the language we use to discuss inner internal states and conditions didn't arrive from the inspection of anything inside other people. We—someone—looked at the exterior of people, gave observable characteristics a name, and then invented inner components to account for the outer manifestations.

The abstract words are extrapolations—or rather interpolations—from concrete observations.

This is the reflective flip once more. We find words to characterize and explain the behavior of others and then reflect them onto ourselves. The inner categories are inventions. Words like *memory, learning*, and *consciousness, happiness, sociability, inventiveness*, were never established to describe anything going on *inside* other people. They were words to describe outward characteristics. But when we flipped these reflective words back onto ourselves, we carried with them the invented inner structures supposed to account for observable behavior.

We're forced to make the reflective flip, even if we don't realize we're doing so, because language does it for us. We have no need to conceptualize the reflective experiences and put them into words because they are already established in language.

In fact language now leads (and misleads) us. The inner person unjustifiably put inside others and ourselves has been consolidated and perpetuated by language—by *part* language. Only *person* language can enable us to avoid the semantic traps.

SUMMARY AND IMPLICATIONS FOR EDUCATORS

Students don't acquire information, store memories, or organize data. They grow. *Thinking, learning, remembering*, and *understanding* are descriptive terms for observable aspects of behavior, not explanatory terms for imagined internal mechanisms. They refer to people as a whole, not to parts of them.

The most reliable cues to student competencies, attitudes, and values lie in the way students can be seen to behave, not in clinical analyses and predictions about their potential. The better a teacher knows a student, the more reliable a teacher's judgment will be. For a teacher who doesn't know a student well, it is better to try to remedy that situation directly than to refer to clinical, sociological, or statistical data analyzing students as a class, a type, or a group.

2

Our Certainties

We take the world for granted, don't we? We accept the world we live in, the technology that surrounds us, and the thoughts we think, as the way things naturally are. The world and the people in it could do with some improvement, but by and large everything is as we expect it to be. It all stands to reason.

But the world we live in today is not the only possible world. In earlier times—a thousand, even a hundred, years ago—the world was totally different. Technology looked different, people looked different, and people thought in different ways. Yet these people, our ancestors, thought *their* world was obvious. They couldn't imagine a different world, certainly nothing like the world we live in today. What stood to reason then does not stand to reason now—and what stands to reason now will not stand to reason in the future. The world that seems so self-evident and obvious to us today will be replaced by different worlds in the future, that will seem obvious to the people who live in those worlds. Those people will look back on our world with amused curiosity. The world we live in isn't so obvious after all. It only looks that way because we think it is.

I am talking about what lies behind our certainties—not about what there is in the world that makes it look self-evident to us, because there is nothing of that nature in the world—but of what it is about us, the individuals who perceive the world, that makes our own particular world so obvious and alternative worlds so alien.

CONSTRUCTIVISM

There is a particular philosophical and psychological point of view behind the way I undertake this venture. It is termed *constructivism*. The constructivist point of view is that nothing we know about the world is given to us. Knowledge doesn't exist outside ourselves, waiting to be uncovered or for someone to deliver it to us in the form of instruction or communication. We have ourselves constructed all the knowledge and understanding that we have. Learning is a perpetual matter of *making sense.*

The constructivist point of view is not the only approach to learning. In fact it is a minority opinion. Most of the instruction that goes on in schools and universities—as well as in educational books and on the Internet—is based on the assumption that learning is the acquisition of knowledge and that knowledge *is* communicable. That is the way you find out things—someone tells you what you want or need to know. It is frequently not easy to communicate knowledge in this manner, though fault is usually attributed to the learner (faulty reception) rather than to the instructor (faulty transmission). This is the reason that so much practice, repetition, assessment, and blame is associated with efforts to get students to assimilate information, to acquire knowledge, especially when delivered on a predetermined schedule. Many educators feel that if you can't succeed in face of a constant barrage of carefully selected information, then you haven't got a hope. You are intellectually, socially, or genetically handicapped.

In the view of such people, we have to learn in order to comprehend anything. My view is the reverse. In order to learn, we have to comprehend. Sense comes first. Learning doesn't make comprehension possible; comprehension makes learning possible. There is in fact no difference between comprehension and learning.

The idea that knowledge has to be delivered in neatly packaged and repetitious drills and exercises has no lengthy historical antecedents. Until education—like farming, manufacturing, and public administration—became systematically organized in the middle of the 19th century, the prevailing point of view had for centuries been that you learn from the company you keep. You're expected to be a farm worker?

You're put to work on the land. A sailor? You're sent to sea. A factory hand, or a miner, or a construction worker? You're put in the company of people who do those kinds of thing. You're expected to learn on the job, not by someone instructing you on the key things that you are supposed to know, but by making sense directly of what is going on around you. It's an apprenticeship view of learning, sometimes characterized as *bottom–up*.

The opposite point of view, which has come to prevail in many aspects of our lives, is known as *top–down*. It is a managerial point of view, which claims (or takes for granted) that learning is best accomplished if someone tells you exactly what you should learn, and exactly when and how you should learn it. The managerial view not only tells you what you should learn every step along the way but also insists that you should stay on that preordained path. If you fail to learn what is required at a particular step, then you should not move on to something that is easier or more comprehensible. Instead you should keep beating your head against a wall until you *master* what the system demands.

The constructivist view is that you learn from personal experience, not from what people tell you or from information you find in books. (You can learn from the *experience* you can have by reading a book—often *only* by reading books—but that is by keeping the company of characters in books, and occasionally the authors of books.)

It might be objected that there are many things we would never have learned unless we were given the information in books or by other people—from telephone numbers to the complexities of DNA. But none of these "facts" would be of any use to us unless we could make sense of them. The understanding has to come first.

A necessity for knowledge to be delivered in predesigned instructional packages obviously isn't the case with infants. No one teaches babies how they should make sense of the world or presents them with the essentials for learning language. How could they, before babies understand language? No one *tells* babies what they should know; they find out for themselves. And they do this not by absorbing knowledge—not by osmosis, as is sometimes disparagingly claimed—but by *constructing* it. They build, in their own minds, a theory of the world.

MORE ABOUT LEARNING

False ideas about learning have become entrenched as certainties because of the managerial philosophy that prevails throughout the educational system. The false ideas have become folklore—that you learn more if you try harder, if you are rewarded for success and punished for failure, if the situation is competitive. All untrue. Learning itself is regarded as a process—a mythological learning process—lodged in the brain with a mythological reading process, writing process, and face recognition process. Calling something a process makes it sound more scientific, more amenable to managerial control.

Learning is growth. It goes on continually, just like breathing, the circulation of the blood, and the growth of our fingernails. These are all conditions of the body, not processes. They go on all the time. Learning is like breathing. If there is a time when we are not learning then we know about it, just as we know about it if something interrupts our breathing. With interruption of breathing we feel suffocation. With interruption of learning we feel boredom or confusion— both aversive states (though we may have learned to tolerate or suppress those feelings).

There's a saying that if at first you don't succeed, try again. That belief shouldn't be extended to learning. If you fail to learn something the first time, you're probably going about it the wrong way. The circumstances are wrong, usually because you're trying to learn by rote (sometimes called *memorization*) something you don't understand. And even if you succeed, you haven't achieved very much. Rote learning isn't learning; it quickly fades. Learning is relating something new to everything you know. It is not filling in an empty slot in your knowledge, it's expansion, growth. Your knowledge grows the way your body grows, not by the addition of new bits, but by the expansion in power of what you are already.

LIVING IN THE FUTURE

We might think we live in the present, because it presses on us so much. We may even feel that most of our life is spent catching up with the present. But this is another illusion. We don't live in the present at all. We live in the future—though always with an eye on the past. The focus of every act and every thought is on a future state of affairs, even those states of affairs that will be entirely confined in our own minds. The basis of every act and every thought is *prediction.*

Our reluctance to live in the present has nothing to do with the technicality that as a fixed period of time, the present does not exist. *Now* is a relative term, measured by the calendar as well as by the clock. Depending on the context, now, or the present, can refer to this instant that you are reading this very word (which word?), or this period of time that you are currently devoting to reading, or this day of which your reading is just a part, or even this month or this year. "Last year I spent all my spare time cycling; now I am walking as much as I can." Or "At present, I am on a low calorie diet (or living in Florida, or studying Italian)." There is no limit to how long *now*, or *the present,* can last.

But more significant in the lives we live than the ephemeral fact that *now* as an instant does not exist is the inexorable fact that however long now, or the present, happens to be, there is nothing we can do about the present *right now*. That part of the present is already happening. It is the future that we must pay attention to.

And please don't ask me how far ahead the future is. If we are working toward a degree, the future is when we graduate, but it is also every step on the academic road before we reach that graduation. If we are playing a card game, the future is every card that we might play, and every card that other players might put on the table or hold in their hand. The future is what we should be concerned with right now.

If we are hoping to cross a road, the future is when we get to the other side. Our aim is to anticipate, to predict, everything that might happen as we cross the road. We want to take into account any vehicles that might be coming along the road before they actually hit us, not when they do. If we are driving to town, we are not so much concerned with where we are right now as with how we will get to our destination and with events that might occur during our journey. We predict every step along the way. Only inexperienced drivers worry about where the car is right now.

We don't predict exactly what will happen—that would be prophesy. We predict what might happen, out of a set of alternatives that are all possibilities. That way we protect ourselves against surprise. We're usually not surprised by anything that happens in our lives, not because we were sure they would happen, but because they fall within the range of expected possibilities. We're very good at this, at predicting what *might* happen, which is the reason we are so rarely surprised by what happens and what doesn't happen in our lives.

There can be short-term predictions and long-term predictions. In fact we make concurrent predictions of varying durations at every moment of our lives. Right now I have predictions, I'm making choices, about the next word I'll write, about how I'll continue this sentence, about what I hope to say in this paragraph, about the topic of this chapter, about the purpose of the book—and about when I can take a break for a cup of coffee. I have a pretty good idea of how I'll spend the rest of the day, of what I hope to do tomorrow, and of my plans for next week.

No doubt I'll have to modify many of my predictions in the course of the next few hours and days, but that is one of the advantages of predictions—they can be flexible. It would be absurd to blunder through life with no predictions at all; we would quickly get into all kinds of trouble. But it would be equally ludicrous to start the year, or the week, or even the hour, with a rigid plan of action that we would never adapt to changing circumstances.

You may notice that the word *predictions* in the preceding paragraph could be replaced with the word *expectations*. Any difference is purely stylistic—a prediction to me is a little more precise, and a little more flexible, than an expectation. But I don't want to suggest that prediction is another one of those fictitious *processes* in the human brain. Prediction—or expectation—is a constant state, a normal part of comprehending the world. We don't make sense of the world by assessing our current circumstances, but by evaluating how well our predictions work out. Our certainties are constructed.

And please remember, I am using *person* language here, not *part* language. When I talk about predictions and expectations, about comprehension, learning, and a theory of the world, I am talking about people, as seen or heard from the outside, not about parts of them assumed to be somewhere in the inside. I am talking about people predicting and learning, not about some device inside them that is supposed to be doing the predicting and learning for them.

EXPLAINING TERMS

I should first clarify a few terms—*comprehension, learning,* and *theory of the world.*

In educational settings, *comprehension* usually refers to a student's ability to answer questions after reading a book, article, or set of instructions. *Learning* is similarly regarded as ability to regurgitate something that has been "taught." I want to broaden the application of both terms, bringing them more in line with their general, out-of-school use.

Comprehension is not in fact a term that is widely used in everyday language. Instead we use the synonymous but less esoteric term *understanding.* We can also use the phrase *making sense* to express the same meaning.

Comprehension, understanding, and making sense—here is my view of what each of the three expressions means: *relating new experience to what we already know.* We comprehend a task, understand what someone is saying, and make sense of a situation, when we can relate what is going on to what we already know—when we have no doubt, uncertainty, or confusion. In other words, comprehension is the way our predictions work out. Comprehension (like making sense and understanding) doesn't apply only to language situations. We can make sense (or fail to make sense) of any aspect of our experience, whether seen, heard, felt, smelled or tasted.

Learning, in many contexts, means the acquisition of something—of facts, data, or information. Acquisition of information is such a passive and superficial view of learning that I prefer to refer to it as rote learning, which I have just characterized as practically useless. Learning integrates new experience with what we already know. It is the possibility of making and evaluating predictions about the future. Learning is not so much bringing something from the outside in as modifying or elaborating what is already inside—the constructivist view. It is adaptation.

I have used exactly the same words to characterize both comprehension and learning—*relating new experience to what we already know.* The repetition was intentional. Just because different words exist doesn't mean that they refer to different things. People tend to think that learning and comprehension have different referents, partly because they have traditionally been used in educational settings to indicate different kinds of intention. There are work books of *learning* exercises and work books of *comprehension* exercises. But these are merely exterior labels, with a false assumption that they somehow refer to different mental activities. The content of such books tends to be the same—read something and answer questions. And the mental activity, I argue, is exactly the same. It is all a matter of making sense, of relating experience to what we already know.

And what is it that we already know to which I continually refer? I call it *the theory of the world* that each of us, including infants, employs as our basis for making sense of the world.

THE THEORY OF THE WORLD

The theory of the world to which I refer is not an appendage to us, carried around in a briefcase or in some internal storage. It is *us*, an aspect of who we are. It is how we make sense of experience (or rather, how experience makes sense of itself). It is the basis of all our certainties.

By theory, I mean an integrated web of knowledge and beliefs. By the world, I mean the totality of anyone's actual or potential (or imagined) experiences. I mean the physical world—anywhere we might travel and stay in our lives, but especially the actual surroundings that we find ourselves in at any particular time. I also mean much more than the physical world—I mean the way other people in those surroundings interact with each other and with us. I mean all the technology in the world and all the institutions—the political system, the legal system, the health system, the educational system, and systems of beliefs and values. Everything, in short, that impinges upon our lives, sources of opportunity and constraint. The world of fish is more than a world of water—it is a world of mud, sand, rocks, coral, and marine vegetation of all kinds, a world of other creatures, of predators and prey. The world of humans is more than a sphere of land and oceans, it is everything pertaining to that habitat that impinges upon our own lives. Language and technology are two aspects of that habitat, as pervasive as the weather.

We don't have to carry a world around with us, complete or in part, in the concrete form of maps, pictures, descriptions, or images of some ecological reality. We don't *know* what the world is like, but we do have ideas. And our ideas are not lying around all over the place, one idea here and another there. All our ideas, our knowledge, our beliefs, our understandings are integrated into a single coherent theory. Why should I call it a theory, rather than just an accumulation of knowledge (or of hypotheses)? Because it serves exactly the same purposes as a theory in science.

Scientific theories have three functions, related to the past, present, and future. The first function is to provide a useful summary of everything the scientist has learned. It takes the place of a long list of unrelated incidents and becomes the scientist's memory, the essence of experience. Scientists don't try to remember data; they look for principles.

These principles in turn influence how the scientist will perceive and interpret new data, the second function of theories. Astronomers who once held to the theory that our universe revolved around the earth perceived the movement of the planets quite differently from Copernicus, whose own theory enabled him to perceive their movement in relation to the sun. All scientists were looking at the same data, the same movement of the planets, but what they saw was determined by their underlying theory of the nature of the universe.

The third function of a scientific theory is to serve as a source of hypotheses about the future. Scientists don't wait passively for events to happen. Instead they construct hypotheses that become the basis of the "experiments" they perform, and they confirm or modify their theories in the light of the experimental results. It is exactly the same with babies and with all humans in every aspect of their affairs—unless they are behaving randomly, which is a most unusual occurrence.

We try to make sense of the world by distilling all our experiences to a theory of the world we have been developing since birth. Just like scientists, we use the theory as a summary of past experience, a way of interpreting the present, and a source of expectations about the future. The theory, constantly tested and modified, is the way we make sense of the world. This constant testing and adapting is what we call *thinking*.

I should add a cautionary note. We can model our theory of the world to any form we desire—not specifically the actual reality (whatever that might be) in which we find ourselves, but a reality richly interlarded with mistaken or imaginary elements. We always get the feeling that the world as we perceive it is the world as it is, but the feeling comes because "reality" is always filtered through our theory of the world—and because other people appear to share a similar reality (or a similar theory).

And because our theory of the world is constructed out of our own experience and interpretations, we are also vulnerable. We cannot ignore our surroundings; in fact we strive to assimilate them, especially in the realm of language and the realm of technology. We may construct our theories of the world, individually and together, but much of the material that goes into these theories comes from an outside world that is not always benign and well-intentioned. Our experience can mislead us, and so can our own desires and predilections. All our certainties are fallible.

A FINAL POINT

One other matter should be mentioned before I delve into the lively world of infancy. There is a tendency among researchers who write about the development of children—*mea culpa*, myself included—to focus on their intellectual achievements. Because it is our primary concern, we write as if the sole activity and impulse of children is to learn about the world.

But children are not mere interpreters of experience. They don't wait to see what happens to them and then analyze it dispassionately. Children are spirited bundles of energy, driven by emotions, desires, hopes, fears, curiosity, determination, and power. They are *people*, and they are individuals. Their urge to make sense of the world is often part of a greater urge to *change* the world, or to assert their own place in it. Children—and adults—are rarely as passive in the hothouse of life as they may seem in the clinical climate of print. Our potential and our experiences lead us all in different directions. We may have the same cognitive equipment, but we aren't clones.

SUMMARY AND IMPLICATIONS FOR EDUCATORS

The constructivist point of view is that nothing we know about the world is given to us. Knowledge doesn't exist outside ourselves, waiting to be uncovered or for someone to deliver it to us in the form of instruction or communication. We have ourselves constructed all the knowledge and understanding that we have. Learning is a perpetual matter of *making sense.*

Students constantly endeavor to make sense of educational practices. Even when they rebel against school, they charitably assume that their teachers are trying to achieve something worthwhile for them. They even believe that continual testing must be good for them. Few students are aware of the rituals and politics that underlie much educational practice.

3

Our Ideas

We were born knowing nothing of the world. As babies we may have had a few instinctive movements and reactions—we didn't have to learn to be startled, or to breathe, or to suckle—but we knew nothing of the world at large. We didn't know that the world contained objects that have a certain degree of permanence and other objects that are transient. We didn't know that many things can move but that others are relatively stable. We didn't know that one thing can cause another. We didn't know that there are other people in the world—or that we ourselves were a person. We didn't even know there was a world, rather than simply an enormous extension of ourselves. Everything we would ever learn lay in the future for us, and even *that* we had to learn. We began with no notion of time, or space, or of ourselves. Every idea had to come from within us. Knowledge of the world was a matter of construction, not instruction. We had to make sense of everything going on around us.

At the beginning we slept for about 16 hours of the day, and for half of the remaining 8 hours we were inactive—lying, watching, thinking. All of our senses were operative, but we had no idea of what any of our senses told us, apart from pleasure or discomfort. We had an intuitive response to the direction of events and would direct our gaze toward movement, a sound, or a smell. Our first motivated actions weren't focused on the outside world at all but on our own bodies. We had to discover that we had arms and legs, hands and fingers, a head and a body, and that these parts could be moved, with intention and precision. Instinct may have urged us to get up and walk, to climb and to jump, but we had to learn how to roll over, crawl, and coordinate eyes, legs, and balance on the way to these goals. We couldn't even roll over until we learned to keep our arms out of the way. We had to *learn* to be walkers, but no one taught us to do this. The most that adults could do was give us support and encouragement.

We were constructive, first about ourselves, then outside. Putting one block on top of another was an exploration driven by a mental intention of seeing what happens if one block is put on top of another. Our behavior wasn't random, although it may have seemed so until we gained control over our limbs.

We needed to learn about gravity. We knew instinctively that we were in danger of falling if we moved too close to an edge, to a "cliff," but we knew nothing of the manner in which objects fall, which explains our lengthy and irritating fascination with dropping things (or wiping them off the end of level surfaces). Repetition was an important part of our learning, not because we liked to do the same thing time and time again, but because each experience extended our knowledge and power.

We were constantly exploring the world with our eyes, looking not so much for how things were similar as for how they were different. Focusing on what we knew was boring; we didn't spend much time looking at familiar images of faces. But show us a *papier-mâché* face with two eyes on the same side of the nose and we would be surprised, our attention would be gripped, demonstrating that we had an expectation of what a face should look like, even in schematic form. We preferred things that were different to things that were the same. A simple melody that became predictable quickly faded into the background of our attention, unless it became part of a game or a bonding experience. But if that melody was changed slightly, we became alert and interested. There was something new to be learned, to be made sense of. We were interested in novelty, not in what we knew already. We wanted *action*—physical and mental.

CATEGORIES

We organized our experience into categories—there were things that could be eaten and things that couldn't, things that floated and things that didn't, things that flew, things with four legs, things with two. Every category contained groups of objects (or events) that could be regarded as similar to each other, yet as different from objects in other categories. Without such differentiation, there could have been no structure for learning. If we treated everything as the same, there would be no basis for appropriate action. If we treated everything as different, there was no basis for action at all.

Where are these categories located? After what I said about memory in chapter 1, I don't want to imply that we have a catalogue of categories stored away somewhere inside us. What happened to the categories is very simple—they became part of us. We have them today. As we grew, mentally and physically, every experience molded us into who we are today, and the categories we established are another aspect of those experiences.

Categories are essential for making sense of the world and of anything else. The need for differentiating experience into categories may be instinctive, but we had to determine the ways in which the categories were formed. The world didn't tell us what the appropriate categories were to base our attitudes and behaviors on; we had to work those out for ourselves (taking into account, of course, other people's attitudes and behaviors). We could not—and still can't easily—construct categories in any formal sense, with specific rules about how things go together. We interact with the world in a categorical manner, but some things seem to be regarded as more appropriate members of a category than others. A pigeon is regarded as more of a bird than is a pelican, and a cod is more fishlike than a skate. For every category there is a prototype.

Categories by themselves are as useless as shoe boxes for organizing things. Categories themselves need to be organized, and the basis of our organization is their relationships with each other. Categories for cats, dogs, and horses were interrelated because they were all animals, and therefore, we later learned, they had bones, hearts, lungs, and other bodily features in common. There could be subcategories for different kinds of cats, dogs, and horses, just as there could be superordinate categories for mammals and for vertebrates. Category systems are a complex hierarchical structure of interlocking categories, the framework on which much of our theory of the world is constructed.

Even before we became mobile, we constructed internal maps. We knew where the door was, and the windows. Later we *found* (we were not taught) our way around our home and its surroundings; we extended our territory to inside the car and to every other location that we came to occupy. It was not only in space that we established structure, we also organized time. We learned *sequences*, the way one thing follows another, and we learned *scenarios*, the way different events are orchestrated. We learned—but none of it was taught. It was all personally constructed knowledge.

After learning to separate ourselves from the world around us, we could reflect on the relationship between the two. We assessed how the world (and other people) could have effects on us, and how we create differences in the world (and in other people). This reflection on what was and what might be was the beginning of imagination and of the internalized action of thought.

Imaginative thought also enabled us to begin to come to terms with our own emotions, to recognize that we had different feelings about different experiences. We began to discriminate the good from the bad (in our terms). And from such thought came social development and the beginning of what would be a lifelong journey through the challenges of what constitutes morality.

All of this began without language—without any kind of language, and therefore without any possibility of instruction. The first months of life was also the time when we began our dramatic journey into language itself, which would soon change every aspect of our life. Language did very little for us initially in terms of communication—infants usually have little difficulty expressing needs and feelings to other people before they have words. But language rapidly opened up to us another world full of challenges, ideas, and opportunities.

Language was less a tool than a universe of ideas, with an enormous influence on the way we organized the construction of ourselves and the world. Language was the way other people, most of them long gone, shared their organization of the world with us.

NO PLACE FOR THE PAST, LITTLE ROOM FOR THE FUTURE

What special role did technology play in all of this infant learning—the car, the plane, the telephone, television, computers? None. As far as we were concerned, everything was natural, a part of the experiential world in which we found ourselves. Categories for "natural" and "technological" only came with language. (Dogs, cats, and other animals never distinguish between natural and technological objects—they take what comes without question of provenance.) But unsuspected though it was, technology played a tremendous role in our early lives. It was so important that I make the topic a complete chapter at the end of this book.

There was something else that also plays no part in preverbal learning—*the past*. History doesn't exist in the mind of an infant. The world as we first encountered it was a world that must always have been, a world of certainty. The world that makes sense, that stands to reason, was the world that existed *then*. The time of our birth was where time started for us. The only past *we* have ever had is the history of our own experience.

BETWEEN BASELINES AND CEILINGS

We learn, we construct reality, throughout our lives. But the reality we constructed at the beginning was a *baseline*, a state of affairs to which everything has since been related. We cope with new experiences only to the extent that they can be related to our baseline view of the world. The baseline can be modified, or reconstructed, to accommodate future experiences, but only within limits. We'll see later that just as there is a baseline, before which nothing could be integrated into a coherent view of the world, so there is a *ceiling*, beyond which it is difficult to make sense of a changing world. Lives are spent in the conceptual space between each individual's baseline and ceiling. Former and future generations would both find it difficult to come to terms with the world we have today.

The historic past was never integrated into our present; how could it be? Our birth was where everything began. Later in life, as a mental exercise, we might try to trace historical threads that have led to our own lifetimes. But these threads have no reality for us. The people of the past were different people (just look at their photographs), and the technology of the past was unformed, developmental. The original Model T Ford was modern once, the last word in personal transportation, but only to people unable to conceive of today's automobiles. To us, the Model T, if we think about it at all, was a transitory or makeshift form, a curiosity, not part of our present experience (unless we happen to own one).

It is difficult to feel oneself part of a world *without* cars, even if we don't have one ourselves. Most people can't imagine a world without television. Young people today can't imagine a world without cell phones. The historic past, if we think about it at all, is a phantom. Our birth was where everything began, including our personal history. The future is where everything stops—when we hit the ceiling of what we are able to relate to our baseline.

LEARNING

The nature of language and the enormous impact it has on our views of ourselves and of the world is a major topic for later in this book. So also is the nature of technology and the influence it has on us. For the moment, I want to extend the discussion of how everyone continues to learn, to make sense of the world, after the first encounter with language.

Learning, as I am using the term, is a matter of continuously making more and more sense of the world, a constructive process that can only come about on the part of the learner. Some people might argue that there are other aspects of knowledge that can only come to us from outside, that we couldn't construct from simple reflection. They are referring to the acquisition of scientific, geographical, and mathematical *facts* and other types of information. We may have to make sense of the statements that Moscow is the capital of Russia and that 7 is the square root of 49. The facts themselves came from outside ourselves, but *we* have to make sense of them.

The acquisition of facts is best regarded as *rote learning*, experience that may not be fully integrated with everything else we know. These disorganized facts become part of us without making a significant contribution to who we are. They are more akin to historical events rather than actual experience, held in the form of propositions, of statements in language, with no necessary integration into our current understanding of the world.

Learning is *growth,* not storage. With proper nourishment—in the form of comprehended experience—the mind grows in the same way that the physical body grows. Nothing is added. Neither the mind nor the body acquires new bits in the course of development. But existing structure is elaborated and grows in power.

Language that is meaningful to us becomes integrated into our construction of the world; it largely determines our construction of the world. Language is far more than a tool that we can usefully employ; it is an environment in which we live. It shapes our lives even more than the weather.

LEARNING IN LANGUAGE

As children, with a very small number of obvious and atypical exceptions, we were surrounded by language. At first we ignored it—we were far more interested in exploring our bodies and our immediate surroundings. Language was like the paint on the walls; it was present, but it played no part in our lives.

When we did begin to pay attention to language, it was to the sounds. At first we were most interested in the sounds we could make ourselves. This was like trying out our arms and legs. There is a universal babble that every infant produces in exploring the range of sounds our vocal apparatus can create. At that stage, it would not have been possible to detect which particular language we would later begin to speak. At that stage, we could have developed into a fluent speaker of any language. Whether we now speak English, Parsi, Mandarin, or any other of the 6,000 languages in the world is not in our genes.

But within a few months, certain sounds were dropped from our infant verbal repertoire, usually for good. We began to produce only the sounds of the people around us—and it would have been possible to anticipate the language we would eventually speak. There were English babbles and Chinese babbles and Arabic babbles. In effect, we constructed the repertoire of the sounds that would be the basis of the first language that we spoke, our "mother-tongue." These sounds reflected with remarkable precision the timbre and intonation of the particular *dialect* we would speak. Infants in the north of England develop different speech sounds from infants in the south; those in New York develop different sounds from those in Los Angeles or in Houston. We could only begin such learning by paying close (but not conspicuous) attention to the speech of people around us. And those differences, our "accent," have in most cases stayed with us throughout our lives. No matter how much we learn and how far we travel, most of us never shake off the telltale indicators of the language of our origin, the sounds we first practiced in the crib.

As infants, we first responded to emotional aspects of speech (as some nonhuman creatures do), to the intimations of love and acceptance, of prohibition and rejection. This perhaps was the dawn of the realization that some of the sounds that people around us made could have specific meanings attached to them, that sounds could be interpreted. These were the sounds of *language.*

From there our attention went on to making sense of the specific sounds that could be related to objects in the environment. We found (constructed) meanings for words like *drink* (meaning "Would you like a drink?" or "Here's a drink"), *toy, bird,* and other terms that our parents might have uttered in a conversational mode, with us and with other people. And as we began to understand such words, we started to use them ourselves.

The mechanics of such meaning construction, the origin of vocabulary development, have been carefully studied. Understanding for babies is often mediated through the eyes. If our mother said, "drink" as she approached us with a drink in her hand, she probably wasn't looking at us—and we probably weren't looking at her. More likely we both locked our gaze on the object being talked about, on the drink. When our mother said, "Here's your toy," she looked at what was in her hand, and so did we. It's what the eyes and hands are doing when people talk that gave us the clue that objects had names, and what those names were.

And when we grasped the idea that objects had names, we went into what child psychologist Melissa Bowerman called a "frenzy" of name learning. We wanted to know the names of every object we could discriminate—and if we hadn't got a name when we needed one, we made one up.

Names do far more than apply labels to objects; they indicate the existence of categories. Infants normally assume that a name applies to a class of objects rather than to a specific one. "Spot" initially was the name of all dogs, all four-legged animals even, until we worked out that it applied to one animal only. What we deduced from the beginning was that some creatures were called *dogs*, that were not the same as other creatures called *cats.* This is the first great generalizable effect that language has on anyone's thinking, far more important than its role in communication and self-expression. Language indicates the categories that the culture has established and shows how experience should be structured. When we became involved with language, the world became a far more complex and detailed place. And the complexity that language introduced couldn't be ignored. Being immersed in language is like swimming in an ocean—the state of the waters establishes the conditions, but it is the swimmer who has to navigate.

Names indicate categories—including perhaps the most significant category of all, *you*, which gets reflected into the all-important *me*. The way other people treat us, especially in the language they use, is the way identity is formed. And the core of identity lies in the relationship between *me* and *you*. There is no way that the structure of language could elucidate the crucial distinction in the reciprocal use of *me* (or *I*), and *you*. All of this, and the additional categories of *he, she*, and *them*, could only be constructed from the inside. The construction starts with *I*—which is how we began to refer to ourselves—"Want it" became "I want it"; "Give it" became "Give it to me"—and radiates out into *you, us*, and *them*.

Other categories apply to abstractions rather than to events and concrete objects. These abstract categories are usually referred to as *concepts* and introduce realities into life that can only be made sense of by a language user. They include notions of what is *good* and *bad*, *right* and *wrong*, *true* and *false*, and—especially for children—*fair*. With language came the possibilities and the constraints of sharing, collaborating, and socially approved competition.

Deliberately or casually, many of us spend substantial parts of our lives trying to find exact meanings for concepts like *good, fair*, and *true*. And exactitude is impossible to find because they are part of oppositions indicated by the logic of language, not by our senses or by physical experiences.

During the early period of our mental development, language remained in the background, a natural but inconspicuous part of the environment. We didn't even learn that we were dealing with language until we encountered the word *language* itself. We weren't aware that language was a system, rather than a tool. Most people go through their lives without explicit understanding of the system that language is. Without special instruction, we wouldn't have been able to distinguish a noun from a verb, a statement from a question, or an active sentence from a passive. We have language, but we don't usually talk about it. You don't need to know about language to learn about language, especially your first one.

Language is all around us and quickly shapes our thought and behavior, our perception of the world. Language governs people rather than the reverse. In that sense language is like technology. We don't just live in a world of "natural" objects and "natural" phenomena, like the weather and the countryside. We live in a world of language and technology—and for many of us, "nature" is usually very far away. Except, that is, for the fact that for much of the time we regard our artifacts, our language and technologies, as part of the natural world.

SUMMARY AND IMPLICATIONS FOR EDUCATORS

All students have their personal histories, but these reach no further back than the beginnings of their own life. Everything before that is at best a story, more often an irrelevance. Young people can't imagine a world that existed before their lives, before the technology they are familiar with. They may look at the cars, planes, and telephones of times before their birth, but they see them only as curios. They are below the student's baseline of understanding. It is difficult to imagine a world without the technology and fashions that existed when we began making sense of the world. The opposite difficulty may occur for teachers as they try to assimilate in their lives new developments that are above their ceiling of understanding.

Subjects like history, geography, and natural sciences are beyond the original experience of students and can only make sense when the individual begins thinking like historians, geographers, and scientists. A crucial role for teachers is to find the individuals, in life and in literature, with whom students can identify.

4

Our Limitations

I must have made us sound like remarkably powerful creatures in the previous chapters, with our continual ability to make sense of the world and to accommodate to its changes. And powerful we are indeed. But we are not all-powerful. There are limits to what we see and hear, limits to what we can remember, limits to what we can learn, limits to how we can think, and limits even to how sure we can be of being right or wrong. It's time to come down to earth.

LIMITS TO PERCEPTION

Let's start with vision. We may feel that if our eyes are open we can see everything going on around us. But this is an illusion that we create for ourselves, totally contrary to the facts. It is a construction, as compelling (and probably as necessary) as the feeling that everything about our body, all our physical, emotional, and mental characteristics, is unified into the coherent and comprehensive whole that we call our *self*. Our feeling of selfhood is so profound and mysterious that I reserve a chapter for the topic later in the book.

Here are three limitations on vision—all of which usually escape our attention:

1. We don't see everything that is in front of our eyes at any one time.
2. We don't see anything that is in front of our eyes immediately.
3. We don't see anything that is in front of our eyes continuously.

1.   The best way to demonstrate that we don't see everything in front of our eyes is to share an imaginary experiment—what scientists call a *thought experiment.* Imagine that I flash on the monitor of your computer a paragraph of English text, something you can easily read and understand. But I'm only going to give you a moment to look at this paragraph. I'm interested in what you can see in one glance, or between two blinks. It doesn't matter if I allow you to look for a hundredth of a second, or for a quarter of a second. What you see is the maximum that you can see at any one time. Ready? Here's the text:

> *Books confused him. When he thought he had grasped one idea he found it expressed differently by another author and refuted by a third. Authors disagreed on interpretations, disputed personal observations, and rejected experimental evidence. Pure thought they found most suspicious. Most claimed to have corrected every error of the past, but none anticipated being corrected in their turn in the future.*

Are you ready? Watch carefully. *Flash.* How much did you see from those five sentences of text I flashed on the monitor? Just *five words.* That's your limit.

You might have been able to see a five-word phrase in the first line or a five-word phrase anywhere else. Perhaps *being corrected in their turn.* But five words is as much as you can manage.

It doesn't matter where you were looking on the screen, or how much you thought you saw. The most you will be able to tell me immediately after is five words. And you won't be able to report any more words if I give you longer to think about it. If you want to see more, I'll have to allow you a second look. (You could test all this with a friend, perhaps with two cards or pieces of stiff paper, one card covering the other with the print on it except for the brief moment of exposure.)

You think the five-word limit is a handicap? Let's try again, this time with the same words I used in the test paragraph, but all jumbled up—say in alphabetical order. Ready? Here are the words—for a fraction of a second:

> *a and another anticipated author authors being books but by claimed confused corrected differently disagreed disputed error every evidence*

experimental expressed found future grasped had have he him idea in interpretations it most none observations of on one past personal pure refuted rejected suspicious the their they third thought to turn when

How much did you see this time? *Two words.* Perhaps *authors being* or any other pair of adjacent words.

If the words I flashed to you made sense, you would have seen five of them. But if they made no sense, you saw only two.

What accounts for the difference? Nothing to do with the eyes, obviously. How much you see depends on what you already know—but even if you know everything as far as language and subject matter is concerned, you'll still only see five words. If you're a learner to whom the language or the subject matter is largely opaque, you'll see only two words. If for any reason you're anxious not to make a mistake, relying too much on your eyes, two words will again be your limit.

That's not the end of the bad news. The two words that you can see may consist of 10 or 12 letters—but that doesn't mean that you can see 10 or 12 letters in a single glance. You may be able to read *authors being* in one glance, but suppose I flashed the same letters to you in a mixed up order. Ready?

a b e g h i n o r s t u

How much did you see? *Five letters.* Why can you only see 5 letters in a glance when they are arranged in random order, but 10 or a dozen when they are in two words? Once again it's because of what you know in advance of the structure of English words. If you know so little about the language or the topic of what you are reading that you can only read it letter by letter, then the most you'll see at any one time is 2 letters.

There's a graphic name for such a condition. It's called *tunnel vision.*

When you were learning to read, especially if the person trying to teach you forced you to focus on individual letters rather than whole words in meaningful sentences, you would often have been in a state of tunnel vision. No wonder that some children find learning to read difficult while others sail through with no trouble. Partly, it's a matter of whether they are put into a condition of tunnel vision.

Tunnel vision can happen to all of us. It isn't limited to print. You can have tunnel vision when you look at a picture or the objects on a desk.

The more you focus on detail, the less you'll see of the scene as a whole. It's a fact of life, of which we're usually blissfully unaware. We feel we see much more than we do—but that's what it is, a feeling, a comforting illusion.

2.   The little we do see in one glance is not available to us immediately. We have to wait for it. The delay may not be very long—about a second, while we decide what it is we've been looking at—but it means that most of the time we are not seeing at all. Three quarters of the time we are functionally blind. For between a hundredth and a quarter of a second our eyes are active, looking out at what is going on, but for the remainder of the time vision shuts down. Of course, we are not aware of this time lapse, of the intermittence of vision, but that is because of our *feeling* of seeing, not the actual state of affairs. Earlier in this chapter, I compared our feeling of seeing everything with our feeling of selfhood, by which everything about us seems to hang together. The feeling of continual vision is in fact part of the feeling of selfhood—we're not aware of what we actually are but of what we think and feel we are.

3.   I've just explained the lag that occurs between the time we look at a scene and the time we experience having seen something. The delay is about a second. This is the time we need to work out what we have seen in the first moments of a glance. We can't see more if we stare. After that first glance we have to refresh our eyes, either by a blink or by a glance in a new direction. We don't see more if we hold our gaze on an object of desire for more than a second; we see less. Vision is not continuous; it is sporadic.

But once again we are not usually aware of this odd, counterintuitive limitation on vision. Our feelings tell us otherwise, and we need a specially contrived demonstration to illustrate the actual situation. We don't sit all-seeing on the peak of Mount Olympus, whatever we think. We peer through the clouds.

There's one other limitation on seeing that should be mentioned, and that's concerned with time. Some things happen too fast for us to see, like the beat of a hummingbird's wings. Other things move too slowly, like the hour hand of a clock or the growth of a child. (We are aware that children become bigger, of course, but not at intervals shorter than about a month—and then we are more likely to notice that their clothes have grown smaller.)

I won't go through the limited range of our other senses. If you want comparisons, contrast your hearing and sense of smell with those of a dog. We do have one interesting listening ability, however, which is that we can somehow lock onto a single voice in a cacophony of voices. Thirty people may be talking simultaneously at a party, but we can usually follow what one person is saying, even if that person is not close to us or talking to us—provided we are interested in what is being said. We also can usually detect when someone anywhere in the crowd mentions our name, just as we would notice if a person we know came into the room, so we must be aware at some level of everything that is going on. We can also lock onto a particular instrument at a concert, putting other instruments into the background.

LIMITS TO ATTENTION

We can never be aware of everything going on around us—there's a limit to how much we can attend to at any one time. That limit is from five to seven things. Our attention span, in other words, is just big enough for us to retain a telephone number from the time we look it up to the time we try to call the number. If we try to focus on more than the seven digits—on an unfamiliar area code, for example—some of the original items will be lost.

To call a telephone number you've just looked up or that someone has told you, you have to keep it focused in your attention. *Rehearsal* is the felicitous technical term sometimes used. If your attention gets distracted while you are rehearsing the number, part or all of the number will be lost. And if it's gone, it's gone— unless your attention can be refocused on it. Attention has to be used economically. (But we've become so good at employing attention frugally that we're usually not aware of its existence, let alone its limitations.)

Attention doesn't stay in one place very long, probably for good reason, so that we don't "hang" like a computer and stay in a daze. Attention dances around continuously, changing focus several times a second. It's like a bird foraging for seeds, constantly interrupting what it is doing to ascertain that nothing else—a predator, for example—should have priority attention.

Despite its limitations of extent and duration, attention has two compensatory advantages. The first is that our attention gets to work immediately. If the telephone number you are looking at is to hold your attention, it does so at once. No need to think about it. In fact, your best strategy is to start punching the number as soon as you can. The second advantage is that anything you are rehearsing in attention is available to you immediately. Either you have it or you don't. Useless to struggle to recollect; if you can't think of the number, it's gone.

One remedy for the transience of attention is to include whatever we are attending to in our theory of the world, integrated into everything we permanently know. Then we'll have whatever we're attending to forever (though we may not be able to remember it when we want to). But there's a severe limit to how much and how quickly we can add to our knowledge of the world and to how long it takes to locate aspects of that knowledge. This takes us into the realm of remembering.

LIMITS TO REMEMBERING

As I have been saying, we can remember without having a storage location called memory. Remembering involves reorganizing particular aspects of our current state of knowledge for particular purposes, locating things we already know. But this is not always easy. Remembering also involves integrating novel experiences into ourselves. How quickly can we grow? Once again there are limits to what can be accomplished.

We can't get immediate access to everything we know, not because it is lost in storage somewhere, but because we just can't lay our hands on it, so to speak, when we want to. It's like being unable to find your car key or your watch; you know it's not in storage, it's in the room somewhere, but you can't immediately locate it. How quickly we can locate something, in our room or among our knowledge, depends on organization. If we know a way to get to what we are seeking, we find it quicker.

And what about adding to knowledge—making experience permanent? This is remarkably slow. It is so slow, in fact, that we can only consolidate a new experience into ourselves once every 5 seconds. For that seven-digit telephone number to become part of us takes over one half a minute, 5 seconds of rehearsal for every digit. Five seconds for every new thing.

CHUNKS OF MEANINGFULNESS

I've been vague about saying how much can be held in attention at any one time, or how quickly new experience can be integrated into ourselves, using terms like *things* and *items*. I should be more specific. When I refer to a *thing*, I should say "the biggest chunk of what you can make sense of." A group of random numbers like 7425136 fills attention because the numbers aren't connected in any way. But the same numbers in the sequence 1234567 would only occupy a fraction of attention span because it is something we know already. The same applies to familiar words and names. The letters *a h o t r s u* would overflow from attention, but rearranged as *authors* they would take up only one position. We probably wouldn't make *a h o t r s u* part of our knowledge because it is unrelated to anything else we know, but the word *authors* is doubtless there already.

The general rule applies here, to remembering as well as to perception: *How well you cope with anything new depends on how much you know already.*

I have used words and digits in my illustrations of attention because they are easy to talk about and quantify. But we have the same kinds of limitations for all our senses.

THE CURSE OF ZEIGARNIK

In Berlin in 1927, a German psychologist named Zeigarnik reported a simple but compelling experiment. She required her research subjects to perform a series of 20 brief tasks, like small mathematical calculations and word searches. She interrupted half the tasks (randomly selected, but always for a plausible reason) so that the subjects were unable to complete them. At the end, she asked her subjects to recall as many of the tasks as they could. And she found that interrupted tasks were recalled over 50% more often than completed ones. The finding was subsequently replicated many times, with greater effects in tasks in which subjects were especially involved or interested.

My generalization is that we are more likely to recall those undertakings that we were unable to complete in the past than those that we were finished with. Why do I call this a curse? Because it means we are more likely to remember things that didn't work out the way we wanted rather than other things that might give us more retrospective satisfaction. We think about the clinching comment we never made, the opportunity we missed, the vacation we didn't take, rather than the actual remarks, decisions, and vacations that would provide more pleasurable reflection. We dwell on the frustration rather than the fulfillment, on what we would have preferred to happen rather than on what did. Imagination trumps reality.

If it weren't for the Zeigarnik effect, many people might be far less moody, broody, vengeful, and bitter.

LIMITS TO LEARNING

Learning a foreign language is often subject to self-imposed limitations. A second language is notoriously the most difficult to learn, and the reason is that when we have finished the complicated and time-consuming task of learning our first language (infants do it remarkably rapidly, but it still takes several years) we have a tendency to think we've finished. We've learned one language, why even consider that there might be others, or that they should be worth bothering about? Besides, we establish our identity in our first language, which forms a substantial part of who we are and how we see ourselves and the world. Breaking into this fortress of self-assurance and self-centeredness is not easy.

The best way to learn another language is to see yourself as a speaker of that language. That's not easy for a person who speaks only one language, but it gets easier for every language you attempt to learn after the second, when the barricades of commitment to your first language have been breached.

Babies born in bilingual environments often have an enormous advantage. They never have the idea that there is only one language in the world, and tackle the pair of languages they first encounter with the same aplomb as infants learning only one. Bilingual children and others who learn more than one language tend also to grow up smarter. It would appear that just one language locks us into fairly rigid modes of thought, while a second opens us up to other worlds, other possibilities.

To learn anything, we must do much more than simply apply ourselves to a learning task. We must identify with people who already have the desired skills or knowledge—"joining the club" is the way I talk about it. We need these people to give us relevant demonstrations, collaboration, and encouragement—or at least, to give us a feeling of participation. If we feel we don't belong in a particular club, whether of speakers of a particular language, mathematicians, sailors, or cybernauts, then it is much harder for us to learn to do what club members do. We feel that this is not the kind of thing we should be able to do, and even worse—a situation that may often have afflicted us in school—some part of us may have actively resisted learning what we were expected to learn. If we don't see ourselves as a particular kind of person, we may make sure that nobody could want to think that we want to be that kind of person. We'll try desperately to be different. Social interaction doesn't always promote constructive learning.

LIMITS TO THINKING

Are there limits to what people can think about? There are many concepts that most people have trouble getting their minds around—like *infinity, eternity, the universe before the big bang, the warping of time and other aspects of relativity theory* and *quantum theory* (where objects can be in two places at the same time, and events take place only if someone is watching). We may be familiar with the heavyweight words I have just used, and might even claim to understand them, or at least be able to offer definitions. But as for visualizing the states of affairs to which these words refer, most of us would draw a blank. Even experts have difficulty finding images for the abstruse situations that they work with, and have to do their thinking and experiments in a medium that they find more compatible with their minds, with mathematics.

Some concepts have defied comprehension since people started thinking about them. We all feel we know what *consciousness* is, and what the *self* is like, because we experience them ourselves. But for explaining them, or describing them, thousands of years have been spent in unproductive contemplation and argument. I have on my own bookshelves a dozen volumes by people with authoritative positions in prestigious universities who claim (often most convincingly) that consciousness is one thing, or a completely different thing, or that it doesn't exist at all. One profound thinker, Noam Chomsky, has proposed that we just don't have the kind of intelligence that could ever understand consciousness. It's a problem the human race is just not equipped to tackle.

The human mind is massively wide but painfully slow. We are at our brilliant best when analyzing what is happening at a particular moment but not so adept at serial activities. That is why we are outstanding at pattern recognition—infinitely superior to computers in detecting differences and similarities in faces, landscapes, constellations, and other complex patterns. But for serial tasks like mathematics, computers beat us hollow. Computers can do simple mathematical problems a million times faster than we can—and with far greater accuracy.

There are limits to how fast we can do anything. We can only produce or understand speech at about 300 words a minute. Anything faster than that—or anything very much slower, for that matter—is not speech we can cope with. Talking faster (or louder) doesn't help anyone understand more.

The dazzling arpeggios of virtuoso musicians are not played one note at a time; the notes must be practiced and mastered in batches, in extended phrases, before they can be run off in seamless sequences on the strings or the keyboard. The faster our vehicles travel, the more technological help we need in controlling them. Life is often a problem of trying to keep up.

We also don't have the kind of mind we need for mathematical situations. I don't mean *doing* mathematics, I mean responding appropriately to mathematical aspects of our lives. Our assessments of chance are a case in point. Offer most of us a $1 wager with a 1 in 10 chance of winning $5, and we wouldn't take it. But offer us a $1 wager with a 1 in 1 million chance of winning $500,000 and we might very well take the chance. We're more likely to bet on longer odds for larger amounts; just look at the rush for big prizes in lotteries. Most people would rather drive than fly, but people are much more likely to die in a car crash than they are in a plane crash. If the roulette ball has come up red six times in a row, many people think they have a better chance on black on the next roll. We would think it unusual, suspicious even, if the seven cards we are dealt in a card game were Ace, 2, 3, 4, 5, 6, 7—yet that sequence is no more unlikely than any particular sequence we were actually dealt, say 2, 5, 7, 8, 8, 10, Queen.

Even when we know the mathematical probabilities, we usually don't make use of them. If we read that there's a 0.05 probability of a side effect from some medication, or that it occurs 5% of the time, most of us are less likely to comprehend what it means to us personally than if we are told that it affects one person in 20. Our best comprehension seems to come from the odds—if we know that there's one chance in 20 that we'll suffer the side effect. You'd expect physicians to be better at this kind of judgment than nonspecialists, but they're not. They frequently overestimate the likelihood that a healthy person has a particular complaint if a test for that condition produces a positive result.

We have no real feel for numbers, except in relative terms. We know that five is bigger than four, but we can't *see* four or five things at a glance, without counting them. We know that a billion is bigger than a million, but we can't visualize a million of anything, let alone a billion. We know that a billion is a thousand times bigger than a million, but we can't even imagine a thousand of anything. We hear that the government plans to spend a billion dollars on one project and a million on another. I can't visualize what that means, except that one project is getting a lot more support than the other. Everything with a number attached beyond one and two stays in the realm of numbers, inaccessible to our senses or imagination.

We also can't imagine anything in more than three dimensions, though multidimensional objects are easy to manipulate mathematically—there's nothing logically impossible about them. Multidimensional objects can easily be represented on computer screens—but we can only see (or visualize) three dimensions at a time.

LIMITS TO LOOKING AHEAD

Something else we can't do very well is plan. I don't mean planning a picnic or our next vacation—although we don't always do that kind of thing very well. I mean making contingency plans for unexpected kinds of things that might happen to us in the future. We don't have very comprehensive plans for what we might do if we are suddenly afflicted by illness, or unemployment, or a natural catastrophe. I'm not talking about the fact that we usually don't like to think about such things, but that even if we do, we don't think our plans through very well. We don't pay much attention to possible consequences of our own future actions, let alone other people's.

I know I've said that we're good about predicting, but that's usually short range and close to home. We don't go far ahead with our predictions, especially in terms of possible ramifications of present plans and expectations.

There's a very good reason why, as Robbie Burns put it, the best laid plans of mice and men gang aft agley. We are not constructed for profound engagement in sequential thought; we're much better at the here and now.

Scientists draw a distinction between *parallel processing* and *serial thinking*. We're extremely good at parallel processing, at considering and integrating information coming in from many sources at the same time. Computers aren't. That's why we are far better than computers at recognizing faces and detecting individuals in crowds, and sorting objects into groups. But we're relatively hopeless at arranging one thing after another, laying out events in time, and making plans that take into account options and contingencies every step along the way. We prefer the straight road to byways and diversions. But this is the kind of situation—serial organization—in which computers excel. Their electronic circuits take them forward rather than sideways. Computers can't write music like humans, but they can beat us at chess. They are better at weather forecasting than we are, and they are better at constructing—and making use of—gambling odds.

Only human imagination leaps freely into the past or the future, and its digressions from the present are more spontaneous than planned.

LIMITS TO CERTAINTY

Well, at least we know whether we're right or wrong, right? Wrong! Was that a raven you saw over there, your friend across the road, the salt you put in the soup, the correct answer you gave to the test question? You may feel comfortably secure in your decision, even certain, but there's always a chance you might be wrong, whether you decide *yes* or *no*. And the odd thing is, the more you want to be sure of being right, the more likely you are to make a mistake.

Here's the classic situation. You're a radar operator on watch for incoming enemy planes (let's say in a computer game). If you spot an incoming plane on your monitor, then you give the order that launches 100 missiles and possibly starts Word War lll. Call that a *hit*, and score yourself a point. If you spot a passing bird on your monitor, you give the order to relax and the missiles remain locked in their silos. Call that a *hit* as well, and score yourself another point.

But suppose you make a mistake? Suppose you think you see a plane and start Word War III, when what was actually on the monitor was a bird. Call that a *false alarm* and deduct a large number of penalty points from your score. Or suppose you think you see a bird and cause everyone to relax, when what was on the monitor was a bomber and you are about to be obliterated. Call that a *miss* and deduct penalty points again.

Ideally, of course, you'll score only hits—reporting planes when there are planes present and birds when there are birds. But we live in a noisy world, full of ephemeral events and unavoidable distractions. There's always a chance of a miss or a false alarm, no matter how much you try to avoid them.

And here's the rub. The more anxious you are to spot the enemy planes, the more likely you are to issue a false alarm. If there's any uncertainty in your mind, you'll err on the side of making a positive identification. This is an inexorable rule: *The more intently you watch for a particular event, the more likely you are to make a false identification.*

On the other hand, if you are reluctant to risk an attack, then the probability increases that you will let an enemy bomber through. That's the other inexorable rule: *The more you strive to avoid false alarms, the more likely you are to miss what you are looking for.*

What determines the ratio of hits to false alarms and misses? Signal detection theorists, who are the specialists who first recognized and studied this eternal dilemma, refer to the *criterion level* of the observer. Observers who want to minimize false alarms set their criterion level high and will only report a hit if absolutely certain. Observers who want to maximize hits set their criterion level low and take the chance of an occasional false alarm.

You can't win. The more important a positive sighting is for you, the more false alarms you'll trigger. But the more cautious you are about false alarms, the more misses you'll incur. You can make changes to your criterion level, but you pay a price in false alarms or misses for every change you make.

Every decision you make involves a possibility of error. Were you really looking at a raven, is that really your friend across the road, was that salt you put in your soup, and was that the correct answer that you gave to the test question? The confidence you will put in being right depends on the embarrassment or sanctions you could suffer by being wrong.

Nothing in life is certain, including certainty itself.

SUMMARY AND IMPLICATIONS FOR EDUCATORS

Every aspect of perception and thinking has its limitations. We are not aware of these limitations in ourselves because we have lived with them all our lives (like the blind spot in the eye) and teachers may not be aware of these limitations in students. It is not difficult to create confusion and bewilderment in others, not because teachers are deliberately trying to push students beyond their capacity, but because teachers aren't aware of these limitations in themselves.

It is easy for teachers—and for writers—to think that what seems totally comprehensible to them must be equally comprehensible to others.

5

Our Differences

I observed at the beginning that though we all have the same kind of intellectual equipment and similar genetic endowments, we're not clones of each other. It would be impossible to find two people, even identical twins, with exactly the same patterns of knowledge, skills, habits, interests, values, hopes, fears, tastes, delights, and regrets. It would be impossible to find two people who think in exactly the same way.

Many differences can be attributed to experience, to our individual histories. But other differences are substantial parts of our physical and psychological makeup, characteristic ways in which we make sense of the world and interact with it. It is these differences, large and small, that make each of us an individual. They are the reason that we all appear to be different from everyone else—and feel that we are different.

Despite these self-evident individual differences, there has been an enormous research effort in psychology to classify people into *types.* The drive to categorize played a major role in the establishment of psychology as a science in the 1850s and had fascinated philosophers for centuries before that.

Once of the biggest differences attributed to people is intelligence—such a large and contentious issue that I'm going to postpone it for a while and examine something much less controversial—*styles,* sometimes called *traits.* I'm not talking of styles in fashion, though they are part of it, but of personal styles. These styles are seen as ways in which whole groups of people differ from each other—or rather ways in which whole groups are "the same."

From a mountain of choices, I'll give just one example of a typical research procedure for a personality style. It's called *field dependence–independence.* The theory and research procedure are best illustrated by describing the experimental situation in which the style is studied.

A PSYCHOLOGICAL FRAME UP

You're seated in a completely darkened room. You can't even see the walls or the floor. All you can see is a picture frame, suspended from some invisible mechanism. Your job is to direct an unseen researcher to adjust the position of the frame so that it is properly oriented to the floor—so that it is horizontal, in other words.

Even with all visual clues removed, there are still two ways by which you could normally make a good job of aligning the frame. The first is the vestibular system in your inner ear that habitually keeps you informed about which direction is up, keeping your body vertically oriented. The second clue to horizontality is the seat of your pants. Even if you can't see the floor, you can use the chair you are sitting on as a frame of reference for how everything is aligned.

Suppose, now, the researcher tricks you in your darkened room and puts you on a chair that is not level with the floor. The two legs on one side of the chair are slightly shorter—though you're not told this. Now you have conflicting clues. Your inner ear tells you that one direction is up, but your chair tells you a slightly different story. Which clue do you rely on to make your judgment about aligning the picture frame?

If you favor the misleading clue from the chair, you are said to be *field dependent*, tending to be influenced by information from the outside world. If you ignore the chair and trust your body, you are said to be *field independent,* not completely swayed by outside evidence. This is a *trait*, an aspect of your personality. The construct is said to have *face validity* (in other words, the test measures what the researcher thinks it measures).

There are several problems with such type casting. All people fall between the two extremes. Completely field-dependent individuals would have no volition of their own and be at the mercy of their environment. Completely field-independent people might be dissociated from reality and live entirely in a solipsistic world of fantasy. And field-dependent people act independently from time to time, while the field-independent still have their moments when their beliefs and behavior are determined by circumstances. You can't rely on people acting in the way they are characterized.

In fact, we could argue that the source of this alleged trait in the personality arises from circumstances rather than from individuals. The trait is less an aspect of people than a consequence of the situations they find themselves in. At best, a trait is a way of describing people rather than of explaining them. And English has thousands of words that can be used to describe people.

THE TRADE IN TRAITS

Nevertheless, the pursuit of summary traits to characterize people, to *stereotype* them, continues. Many other traits have been proposed and studied.

Here's an incomplete list of examples. I don't want to group them in any way that might suggest interrelatedness, or relative importance, so I'll simply put them in alphabetical order:

Altruism
Approach/avoidance (with respect to challenges and conflicts)
Authoritarianism
Cheerfulness
Conformity
Cooperativeness
Curiosity
Daydreaming
Dominance/submission
Drug dependence
Honesty
Impulsivity
Introversion/extraversion
Irritability
Leveling (smoothing out differences) versus sharpening (magnifying differences)

Modesty
Neuroticism
Optimism
Talkativeness
Thoughtfulness
Timidity
Tolerance for instability and ambiguity

We've all seen these kinds of behavior in others from time to time and possibly have detected some in ourselves. So what is wrong with the list?

The characteristics are usually seen by other people rather than projected by the individual concerned. They may have nothing to do with behavior as such, but only with the way other people perceive the person. The traits may be imposed rather than expressed. They are arbitrarily selected descriptions of people.

There is no evidence that any of these characteristics are *in* people, as opposed to being observable in behavior, nor can any of them be said to *cause* behavior. Optimism doesn't cause people to talk and behave in optimistic ways. People say or do optimistic things.

No one behaves in any of these ways all the time—a lawyer who is cautious in court may be a reckless driver on the way home. A teacher may be a Jekyll at school and a Hyde at home—or vice versa.

What are the determinants of traits—or characteristic ways of behaving? There is a mélange of factors, ranging from the inherited (genetic predispositions) to life experiences—in family, among friends, in workplaces, in schools, in cultural and social value systems, and in economic circumstances. Potent experiences for many of us come from books, movies, television, and plays, and from our own imagination. No two people could have identical experiences, even along just one of these dimensions. You and I could smell the same flower or drink the same wine, but our experiences would differ because of our entire lives spent as unique individuals, no matter how much we may share interests.

Mathematicians and statisticians can't begin to calculate the total of possible combinations and permutations of traits. But it is clear that the number of alternatives is more than sufficient to make every person in the world a unique individual. The mathematics show there could be more distinctive individuals on earth than there are stars in the universe.

Here's a simplified calculation. Let's take the 20 traits I listed previously, from altruism to tolerance for ambiguity. And let's say that any individual can be at any one of 10 positions on these traits (actually, of course, there are many more positions). Thus for one trait there are 10 possibilities and for 20 traits there are $10 \times 10 \times 10 \times 10 \times 10 \times 10 \times 10 \times 10 \times 10 \times 10 \times 10 \times 10 \times 10 \times 10 \times 10 \times 10 \times 10 \times 10 \times 10 \times 10$ possible combinations, which equals a total of 10^{20}, or 100,000,000,000,000,000,000 possibilities. That's 100 billion billion billion possibilities. These figures are up in the astronomical range—there are a few hundred billion stars in the Milky Way, and a few billion other galaxies in the known universe. Multiply them all together and you have something on the order of the number of variations that are possible for individual human personalities. Of course, the same abundance exists for possible combinations of physical features and even for faces alone.

The amazing thing is not that we are all different, but that we should ever be tempted to regard groups of people as the same and therefore worthy of being stereotyped and even discriminated against.

IN SEARCH OF INTELLIGENCE

Now what about intelligence? *Intelligence* has been cynically defined as what intelligence tests measure. I suggest it is what we choose to call intelligent. It is better considered as a style, even a complex trait, rather than a capacity.

However intelligence is formally defined, people who are supposed to be intelligent according to any definition (and even when measured by purportedly validated tests) can behave in unintelligent ways in different circumstances and even on different occasions. I couldn't claim to be intelligent when I try to make technical repairs on my car, and on some occasions I can be downright stupid. My mechanic has such a first-class intelligence when it comes to my car that it's almost a relief to me to see him make a fool of himself when he endeavors to write out the bill. We may all be reasonably intelligent when it comes to doing our jobs and engaging in our hobbies and pastimes—specific kinds of intelligence are job requirements for most occupations. But then, much of our particular kinds of intelligence probably came from our jobs in the first place.

An intelligent chef may not be an intelligent restaurant manager, and an intelligent manager may be a most unintelligent chef. Many successful restaurants have been founded on such a complementary basis.

Intelligences have been multiplying in recent years, even within single individuals. Where many psychologists were content to classify individuals, cultures, entire nations, and peoples on the basis of just one kind of intelligence, now each of us is supposed to have (or lack) intelligence on a number of independent dimensions. Locked within us are supposed to be relatively stable degrees of intellectual, musical, ethical, practical, and other forms of intelligence.

And so it goes on, the pursuit of the nature of intelligence and the degrees of its manifestation in individuals. All the research shows that circumstances determine who has intelligence and when.

Are animals intelligent? Of course they are, in their own ways in their own worlds. They wouldn't have survived in their harsh world without intelligence. Evolution has ensured that. Animals aren't intelligent the way we are intelligent, but they don't live in our world. We aren't intelligent in the way they're intelligent. I suppose there could be an occasional stupid robin that can't make a good nest or a reindeer that loses its way on the annual migration. Lack of intelligence for them would be far more devastating than it is for us.

LEARNING BY EYE AND BY EAR

There's another way in which people are said to differ *en masse*—in whether they're *visual* or *auditory learners.* Visual learners are supposed to learn better from reading or from looking at movies. Auditory learners are better at hearing people talk. So the theory goes.

Once more, I don't think the topics under discussion are *capacities.* Everyone who can see is a visual learner and everyone who can hear is an auditory learner. Everyone who can both see and hear is a visual *and* auditory learner. No one could have learned to talk if they were not both visual and auditory learners (and people who are physically incapable of seeing or hearing can learn in other ways too). No one grows up thinking

"I'll only learn through my eyes" or "I'll only learn with my ears." The very idea is absurd.

If we're talking about anything at all here, it is about *preferences*, not abilities. Of course some people like to spend time reading or listening to stories and songs, while others enjoy spending time viewing movies or looking at pictures. But not because they are different types of people—only marketing executives need think like that—but because the word *idiosyncratic* applies to all of us.

The only conclusion to be drawn from all the research efforts to identify and classify types is that people are different. We know that. But people differ as individuals, not as members of categories. If we are to be pigeon-holed, there has to be a pigeon-hole for every person.

SUMMARY AND IMPLICATIONS FOR EDUCATORS

Intelligence is a descriptive term for behavior rather than an explanatory term for people. Each one of us can be intelligent in matters with which we are experienced and familiar but unintelligent in others. You may be able to repair a car engine more efficiently than I can, not because you are more intelligent, but because you know more about car engines.

Students are frequently characterized as deficient in intelligence because they lack experience—or interest—in the rituals of school. It is not difficult for teachers to regard students as deficient in intelligence if they have failed to engage in the educational world. Many tests have been devised to facilitate the precise degree to which students should be regarded as intelligent or unintelligent, depending on their compatibility with the world of education.

6

Our Stupidities

A major aim of this book is to examine why people who can be so smart, compassionate, and loving—meaning all of us—can also on occasion behave so stupidly. I should explain what I mean.

The dictionary definition of *stupidity* focuses on seemingly permanent mental characteristics: *slow of mind, obtuse, dull in feeling, unreasoning, given to unintelligent decisions or acts.* These definitions all imply that the term *stupidity* (or *stupid*) applies to individuals who consistently behave in a "slow, obtuse, or dull" way. And that is not my concern at all. I doubt whether there are any real people who behave in the consistently half-witted manner proposed by the dictionary. Instead, I am concerned with the fact that humans, individually and in groups, are in certain circumstances capable of what I would term stupid behavior—specifically, cruel and brutal acts.

A few people may be like this genetically or as a result of illness—but I'm not talking of the clinical or pathological cases. I'm talking of *ordinary* people, like you and me, who can be smart and loving most of the time, especially among their friends and families, but who occasionally behave in cruel and callous ways, sanctioned by senseless attitudes and beliefs.

I am not talking of mundane events, when we might berate ourselves as stupid for mislaying a key or putting a ding in the car, mistaking mustard for marmalade or sugar for salt. Such incidents could more charitably be regarded as carelessness rather than stupidity.

Here's the kind of thing I have in mind: the organized slaughter of war and the chaotic havoc of the odiously named ethnic cleansing, the maltreatment of the helpless, physical or mental violence, deliberate starvation or neglect, lack of compassion for those in need, disregard for victims of accidents and other traumatic events, ruthless competitiveness and excessive selfishness. This is the kind of conduct that I am characterizing as stupid—behaviors that do otherwise sensible people no credit.

THE EXTENT OF STUPIDITY

We should perhaps begin with a sense of proportion. *Stupidity* as I am defining it is not as widespread as we might think, exceptions rather than the rule. Abhorrent behavior might not occur as frequently as the media would lead us to think, because the media are more likely to publish harrowing or exceptional events rather than the quietly commonplace.

One war is too many, and so is one crime. But notions that the world is plagued by war and riddled with crime are excessive. Most of the world lives in peace most of the time, and many people go through their lives without experiencing—and certainly without engaging in—crime. Peace is not news (except for its pursuit in the context of war), partly because there is so much of it. We take peace for granted; it is the usual state of affairs, and we are shocked by stupid infractions.

SOME COMMON JUSTIFICATIONS

One explanation for stupidly callous attitudes toward others is that we are more naturally concerned with things nearer to home. Distance is supposed to lend enchantment while familiarity breeds contempt, but the reverse is the case. Distance dulls sensitivity. A minor flood in your hometown gets more local media coverage and general interest than a catastrophic inundation on the other side of the world.

Another common explanation is that sensitivity declines with overexposure—we can look at just so many starving faces before we become inured to them. There is nothing we can do except write an occasional check. Some dedicated people do far more, organizing aid and sometimes traveling to afflicted areas to bring help and support to victims. But even they are limited in what they can do. A lifetime's dedication to one cause entails a lifetime's neglect of all the others. To worry about the plight of everyone in the world would be pathological.

In times of armed conflict, even if we are not personally involved in the killing and maiming, we are more concerned with casualties on our own side or on the side we sympathize with, than we are with casualties on the other. Once again, media coverage reflects this imbalance.

Underlying all of these attitudes is the way we identify ourselves and identify others, the primal division of the world into *us* and *them*. The analogy I used earlier of "joining the club" to describe how we achieve identity necessarily entails that there are people who aren't members of the club, with whom we definitely don't identify. On both sides of the dichotomy we raise a superstructure of "facts" to differentiate us from them, generally positive on our side and negative on the other but often extreme and senseless.

I'll begin with a pair of attitudes that are usually found together—*discrimination* and *stereotyping*. We can then see how *prejudice* may be a natural consequence of discrimination and stereotyping, and that prejudice leads inevitably to *intolerance*, which is the underlying basis of all senseless facts and stupid acts.

DISCRIMINATION

We discriminate all the time, of course, to distinguish everything in our lives, birds from trees, trees from bushes, bushes from grass, the edible from the noxious, the drinkable from the emetic. We couldn't live an organized life without discrimination of objects, events—and people—into categories. We need to be able to distinguish podiatrists from pediatricians, chartered accountants from charlatans.

I described in chapter 1 how infants begin to sort their experiences into categories, in order to impose sense upon the world, and how this natural process is augmented by language, which introduces many thousands of new categories into which aspects of experience can be allocated. Language carries the experience of all the world's past inhabitants forward.

We are faced with a universal choice of establishing huge numbers of categories with a few members in each (such as the cases where individual elements have personal names—Pam, Dick, and Harriet)—or a smaller workable number of categories, each of which can accommodate many members with a group name—(footballers, Republicans,

Scots). And the universal solution is to have relatively few categories with membership restricted to one or a few, and a larger but manageable number of categories each with many members.

The simple act of discrimination itself is necessary and unobjectionable behavior. But the word has acquired negative connotations because exclusionary attitudes are often directed toward a particular group that is selected out—when *discrimination* becomes *discrimination against.*

STEREOTYPING

The word *stereotype* originally referred to a metal plate for printing the same image time and time again; it now means (according to one dictionary definition) a standardized mental picture that is held in common by members of a group. Everyone is different, but we stereotype people because we can't deal with or think of everyone in different ways. We stereotype the people we discriminate against.

The dictionary also goes on to note that a stereotype can represent an oversimplified opinion, prejudiced attitude, or uncritical judgment. And this is the problem with the useful words *discrimination* and *stereotyping*; they have acquired negative connotations. Both are seen in a context of *prejudice.*

PREJUDICE

The word *prejudice* itself has acquired a negative tone that it never originally warranted. Once a legal term referring neutrally to earlier judgments, "prior justice," it became a term for a negative state of affairs long before it was regarded as a description of someone's attitudes.

Prejudice is as natural as prediction; in fact the two dispositions come from the same source, the need to anticipate the future before it unexpectedly overwhelms us. Prejudice isn't necessarily intolerance, but intolerance always involves prejudice, in its negative sense.

INTOLERANCE

Problems arise when discrimination, stereotyping, and prejudice are accompanied by *intolerance*. Intolerance energizes prejudice. There are things—and people—we can't stand, and we have to show it.

Intolerance is exacerbated if we can't understand what people we are prejudiced against are saying, if they decline to share our language. They refuse to join *us*—and consolidate themselves as *them*.

Of course, what I've been saying doesn't apply to you and me—but it applies to many others, even to people who would deny having a discriminatory thought in their head. It applies to people who begin a remark by saying, "I'm not racist, but ..." or "Some of my best friends are ...."

As individuals, newcomers are often welcomed, not seen as any kind of threat—provided they "integrate," becoming part of *us* rather than staying *them*. But the situation is different if they arrive on the scene in numbers; living in the same geographic areas; opening their own shops, churches, and schools; establishing their own newspapers and television stations; electing their own political representatives; speaking their own language; displaying their unfamiliar writing; pursuing their traditional internal conflicts; and becoming prominent and prosperous. In short, if they establish their own community inside yours, like an unwelcome growth, remaining *them* in the heart of *us*.

Intolerance is not exhibited toward individuals who enter our lives on our terms but rather to entire groups. People ask: Why didn't *they* stay in their own country if they didn't want to be like us? They are invaders, not guests. They take advantage of our country and its services but contribute nothing. *They don't belong here.*

The intolerance becomes solidified into senseless facts—these people can't be trusted, they are lazy, they stick together; they are unhealthy, ignorant, subversive; they are a threat.

And senseless facts spawn senseless acts, inflamed by fear, jealousy, territoriality, intolerance—and constant irritation.

FROM ATTITUDES TO IDEOLOGIES

Intolerance is not an all-or-nothing affair. We can be intolerant of large things and intolerant of small things, with outside groups and with friends and family. Our intolerance can range from major resentment to mild annoyance. The scale of the intolerance often bears little relationship to the significance of the intolerable event—a routine inquiry by a telephone marketer about the kind of day we've had may irritate us more than a major mishap with an expensive appliance (especially if our day hasn't been all that great).

Intolerance is also rarely a personal affair; it is unusual for one person's antipathies not to be shared by others around. In other words, intolerance is a social phenomenon. It can be difficult for individuals not to be intolerant when the majority in the neighborhood take certain aspects of intolerance for granted. And shared intolerance becomes an ideology—a consolidation of stupidity—with irrational assertions, theories, and aims transformed into sociopolitical programs.

SENSITIVITY

Once again, *ideology* was once a neutral term, referring to any systematic body of concepts, especially about human life or culture, characteristics of individuals or groups, a collection of beliefs to live by. But senseless ideologies, especially those with a nationalistic or racial basis, have made *ideology* itself a suspect word. And the combination of ideology and anger, frustration, and passion, especially when based on unchallengeable religious, political, or social "truths," can be lethal.

Intolerance can result in both an increase and a decrease in sensitivity. On the one hand, we become quick to react to things that impact on us, even when their effect is slight and inconsequential. On the other hand, we are less sensitive to the feelings of other people. Egotism is up; empathy is down; stupidity reigns.

The cure for intolerance has to be a readiness to see all sides of any situation. Tolerance can be learned but from example rather than from instruction, a matter of good models in schools and communities rather than of items on a curriculum. Tolerance could be as infectious as intolerance, if an equal number of models were on hand.

If we don't listen to all sides with equal respect, we become prejudiced. We take it for granted that our side is always right, so it doesn't really matter what happens to the others. Out of intolerance and prejudice, senseless facts are constructed and stupid acts performed.

SUMMARY AND IMPLICATIONS FOR EDUCATORS

Stupidity is a term better applied to actions than to people. It is not as widespread as many people think, and few people exhibit stupidity most of the time. Stupidity is most likely to occur in unfamiliar situations, in the face of unreasonable expectations.

It is easy for all students at one time or another to appear stupid in educational contexts, and easy for teachers and other educators to appear smart. People functioning above their level of competence in educational hierarchies have particular opportunities to commit and cloak stupidities.

7

Our Language

At first glance, it might seem that there can't be much of a problem explaining our ability to understand language. If we've learned the language in our infancy and can hear what someone is saying (or can read what they've written), then obviously we can understand. We know the words, we're familiar with the grammar, so what could go wrong?

But linguists and psychologists have long recognized a fundamental flaw in this uncomplicated point of view. We often say or write things that have two or more meanings, like *the chicken is too hot to eat*, or *she dives into the spray and waves*. Puns are plays on words with more than one meaning, and they aren't always appreciated (another pun). And a meaning can often be expressed in two or more ways, like *unmarried man* and *bachelor*, or *larceny* and *theft*.

So there isn't a simple one-to-one relationship between what we say and what we mean. There's more to language than meets the eye or the ear.

TWO FACETS OF LANGUAGE

The fact that meaning is not always unambiguously represented in what we say has led theorists to drive a wedge between the sounds of speech (or the alphabetic signs of writing) and meaning. Special names have been given to the two aspects of language, the *surface structure*, which is the physical event, and the *deep structure*, which is meaning. The theorists agree that—to use the jargon—there is no one-to-one mapping between the two, between sounds and meaning. (I'll stop talking about writing for a while; exactly the same considerations apply to both spoken and written language.)

The terms *deep* and *surface structures* have been part of a linguist's toolkit for 50 years, and I've made great use of them myself. But I'm no longer sure they are the best way to think about language. They suggest that language is actually split in two—a physical part that has no meaning and a meaning part that has no substance. The language we hear becomes as monumentally incommunicative as a large rock on the shore, with meaning a frail jellyfish peeping out from underneath.

I think it is better to regard the sounds of speech as part of the world around us, fabricated by people with communicative intent but, like every other aspect of the physical world, something we have to interpret. Physical aspects of language aren't superficial or "surface structures" in any way; they are as tangible and substantial as any other physical phenomenon, all there is between one person and another if communication through language is to take place.

Meaning, on the other hand, doesn't float in the air around us. To reiterate the theme of this book, meaning is something that we as individuals *construct.* Forget a special relationship between meaning and language. Meaning has a special relationship with *every* aspect of the world; it is the way we make sense of the world. Nothing is obvious, everything has to be interpreted and made sense of, and the product of that endless process of making sense, of learning and comprehending, is meaning. Meaning is our theory of the world; without it we have nothing.

The difference between *deep structure* and *surface structure* is not a matter of levels but of locations. Deep structure is meaning, constructed by people. Surface structure is in the external world, as acoustic waveforms, and has no sense other than what we give it. The difference between deep and surface, on the one hand, and the world and ourselves, on the other, is more than a change of metaphor. It is a change of view, a shift from metaphor to reality. The part of language that we have to interpret is outside us, a structure in the world, and the meaning that we make belongs only to us, as people. There is nothing metaphorical about that.

MANUFACTURING MEANING

So why concern ourselves with language in this book? Language in the world is patterns of acoustic energy that few of us have any interest in.

Language to us is the sense we make of those patterns. What is there to talk about?

The first thing to note is that we don't hear the sounds of language that come to our ears from outside. What we hear is influenced by the meaning that we attach to those sounds. Here's an example. If I said to you that I live in the west end of the city, you'd have no problem hearing and understanding that the part of the city in which I live is the west end. But listen carefully. I didn't say *west end*, with a pause between the *west* and the *end*. If you repeat the phrase to yourself, you'll find that what is actually said is a completely different pair of sounds, *wes* and *tend*, with a pause between the /s/ and the /t/. *West end* is what you heard because those are words in your language. But for physiological reasons completely unrelated to language, the sounds I actually produced (without knowing it) were *wes tend*. You didn't hear what I said—you heard what I meant.

Speakers of other languages have difficulty detecting the words we actually use in English because we don't pause between every word and we often pause inside individual words. We can distinguish all the words we use, not because there are neat spaces in sound around them but because we already know what the words are. When we listen to a language that isn't familiar to us, then we find it impossible to say what the individual words are. All languages are the same in this respect; their speakers run words together—even when they're "speaking clearly"—and scatter pauses indiscriminately depending on the way they have to articulate the words.

THE TROUBLE WITH WORDS

So what is a *word*? That's another problem. No one can say what a word is, not even a linguist. Before we could read, we weren't aware of words. Even now that we can read, we sometimes run words together in writing the way we say them, like *alot, afterall,* and *gotcha! Altogether* was originally two words whose union has been legitimized. Some words have taken as their correct spelling the historically incorrect way they are spoken. The word *apron* was originally *napron*, but the slight pause in saying *a napron* was shifted forward, to *an apron*, a change reflected in speech and in writing. *Today* was once two words and so was *tomorrow*.

Linguists can't say what a word is because there's no such thing as a word in spoken language. Words arrived on the scene, quite arbitrarily, with written language. Printers wanted to know what words were so they could put spaces between them.

Here's what my dictionary says a *word* is: (1) something that is said (which doesn't explain anything); (2) a sound that communicates a meaning without being divisible into smaller units capable of independent use (which is clearly wrong—many words, like *headache, broadloom,* and *automobile* can clearly be divided into smaller meaningful parts); and (3) units of writing with a space (or punctuation mark) on both sides. And there at last is the answer—words are units of *written* language; they have a space on either side. When you can read, you know what a word is; spaces are conveniently put around it. But the spaces aren't put there because they surround a word. The word becomes what it is because it is surrounded by spaces.

So why do I keep using the word *word*? Because it's a conventional part of speech.

Everyone has a workable meaning for the word, even if they can't define it. The important thing about language is the way we use it, not how we can talk about it. The matter is only worth discussing now as an illustration of how remarkable people are, and as another example that what seems obvious is not necessarily the case.

Back to the linguist's dilemma. You will often hear that a word is a self-contained unit of meaning. But that assumes there is such a thing as a unit of meaning. Most words contain more than a single meaning. Bachelor means unmarried man, but it doesn't follow that unmarried and man have only half a meaning each. Sometimes a word doesn't have a meaning itself, though it adds to the meaning of any word it's attached to, like *very*. To be ill is one thing, but to be very ill is another.

Units of meaning *are* part of the linguist's lexicon. They are called *morphemes*. The word *farmers*, for example, consists of three morphemes, three units of meaning—*farm* (for the activity,) *er* for a person engaged in the activity, and *s* for the plural. *Unhappy* has two morphemes, one for *happy* and the other for its negation. *Child* is one morpheme, and *children* two. *Sheep*, in the singular, is one morpheme, but *sheep*, as a plural, is two. The notorious word *antidisestablishmentari-*

anism contains six morphemes, six meaningful parts. Meaning is not packaged neatly into words.

I mentioned that most words have more than one meaning. I don't mean a few odd or idiosyncratic words but the most common words of the language. In fact, the more common a word is, the more meanings it will have. We like to get the most work out of our favorite tools.

Think of any common word—and see how many meanings it has, how much space it takes up, in the dictionary. Words like *table, chair, dog,* and *fish* all have several meanings. If you want words with just a single meaning, you have to look for the unfamiliar ones, like *illocutionary, intercalary,* or *iridescence,* to stay in just one area of the dictionary.

All of the overworked words not only have a multiplicity of meanings; they may have several grammatical functions. Words like *table, chair, dog,* and *fish* can be verbs as well as nouns, or adjectives, or all three. How can you discover what their meaning and grammatical function is? Only by hearing them in a sentence. Words don't give meaning to sentences; sentences give meanings to words. Most common words by themselves are essentially meaningless.

Here's a simple test I know you'll fail. Say the word *house* aloud. I'm sure you gave the word a noun pronunciation, as in "This is my *house.*" But the word I had in mind was a verb, as in "Who shall *house* the homeless?" Did I trick you—or did language?

Some of the most common words in our language have so many meanings that it's better to say they have no specific meaning at all. I'm thinking of prepositions. I'm sure you have no problem understanding me if I say, "By chance, I found the book by Charles Dickens that you mislaid. It was by the bus stop. I'll send it to you by mail by Friday." I used the word *by* five times, and you undoubtedly understood it five times. But what does the word *by* mean?

By has 39 meanings listed in the Oxford English Dictionary, and so has *at. In, up,* and *with* have 40 meanings listed, and *of* has 69. The meaning of prepositions is so elusive that it is impossible to translate them word for word. They are idiomatic and only earn their living by being part of phrases. To translate *by* into French, you have to consult a list of French idioms. The same difficulty applies in translating French prepositions into English. Many languages get by (another use of the term) with no prepositions at all.

There are many other words that play important roles in language without having any detectable meaning in themselves, like the articles *a* and *the* and the demonstrative pronouns *this, that, those.* They have to be among other words to serve any purpose at all.

THE SENSE OF SENTENCES

So how do we make sense of words, to the extent that we are usually quite unaware of all this potential ambiguity? The answer is by the back door, by making sense of sentences. Words get their meaning from the sentences they are in, and sentences get their meaning because we put it there.

I have to make a disclaimer here about using the word *sentence*, just as I did for the word *word.* Strictly speaking, sentences don't exist in spoken language. They come from writing. Once again, printers are responsible. They not only wanted to distribute spaces to organize text into words, they wanted to include punctuation to organize groups of words. Punctuation has no role in speech, though many people think it does. And many people try to teach punctuation by referring to aspects of spoken language.

So what is a sentence? A typical (and very good) answer is something that begins with a capital letter and ends with a period (or some other form of end punctuation). But this is in written language. There are no capital letters or end punctuation in speech, and we don't normally talk in complete sentences.

There's a romantic view about pauses in and between sentences when we speak, based on the assumption that spoken language is the same as written language, delivered in a similar way. Punctuation is supposed to be present in speech, short pauses representing commas and long pauses representing periods. That is how punctuation is often taught. But the idea is totally wrong. The pause where a comma might be expected, in the middle of a sentence, is usually much longer than the pause at the end of the sentence, and for very good reason.

We put pauses anywhere we want in a spoken sentence while we think about what we might say next, or what we have said in the past, or what someone else has said (or even if we're wondering whether the coffee is ready). The reason we pause in the middle of sentences rather than at the end is a consequence of a very powerful social rule: *No one can interrupt us in the middle of a sentence.* If *you* want to say something, you have to wait until I have finished my sentence.

And that's the reason pauses tend to be short at (pause) the end of spoken sentences, why one sentence runs directly into the next. We don't want to give the other person a chance to interrupt. But we can pause for as long as we like anywhere else in a (pause) sentence, because no one with the slightest respect for good manners would dare interrupt at that (pause, pause, pause) point.

On the issue of punctuation, we were often told in school that we should start a sentence with a capital letter and end it with a period, which our teacher no doubt thought was helpful. But if we had asked the teacher what a sentence was, so that we could dutifully follow those rules, we would no doubt have been told that a sentence was something that started with a capital letter and ended with a period. Completely circular, of course, but what else could a teacher do? There is no other definition of a sentence. An alternative suggestion is sometimes made that a sentence is a complete thought—but can't a sentence contain two or more thoughts? Or sometimes just half a thought?

Most of these schoolroom definitions are empty slogans. They have to be learned to demonstrate competence, but they don't mean anything. Write a paragraph, please. What is a paragraph? A paragraph is a collection of sentences on a single topic or theme. But what is a topic or theme, and how do I recognize one of them? Sometimes a paragraph is just one sentence. Other paragraphs run over pages. The use of paragraphs seems to be quite idiosyncratic among authors, more a matter of personal style and rhythm than of grammatical structure.

If you're an experienced reader and writer, you probably know how to write in paragraphs—you can do it even if you can't talk about it. And if you can't do it, you won't learn by talking about it; you'll just have to do a lot more reading, to assimilate—to *construct*—the way more experienced people do it. You have to join the club of writers, of people who read as if they were writers.

So what does all this business of the complexity and ambiguity of language mean? In practical terms, nothing. We cope. But it does make the constructivist point that nothing comes free in this life. Knowledge doesn't exist outside ourselves, waiting to be invited in, delivered, or internalized through osmosis. We make our own knowledge—and we are very good at it, so much so that most of the time we take it all for granted.

COPING WITH AMBIGUITY

It may seem remarkable that we ever understand what language is about, given the constant ambiguity that exists within it. But we are so good at coping with ambiguity that usually we are unaware that it exists at all. What enables us to pick our way through mine fields of misunderstandings? The answer is that trusty old friend that gets us through so much of life—*prediction*. Prediction indicates the way the sense of language is going, in writing or in speech, and so it protects us against ambiguity. Because we anticipate the direction of a particular piece of language, potential ambiguity doesn't usually worry us at all.

Prediction, as I discussed in chapter 1, protects us from confusion and uncertainty. Prediction enables us to construct a complex theory of the world—to make sense of the world—in ways that usually are relevant to the situation we are in. The same applies to language. Prediction enables us to follow a particular thread of sense in a conversation or a book without pursuing blind or inappropriate alleys.

Sometimes prediction can lead us astray: *Cinderella could not go to the ball—there were tears in her dress.* But our predictions are usually accurate, so much so that we are not aware of how much we use them and depend on them.

SUMMARY AND IMPLICATIONS FOR EDUCATORS

Language is more than a system of communication. It is a complex structure of beliefs, values, ethics, and desires. No two people speak exactly the same language or interpret passages of spoken or written language in exactly the same way. Consensus can be found for the meaning of any utterance, but only to the extent that individuals share a view of the world.

Language is a badge of identity. The hardest thing for any teacher to attempt is to change the way a student talks. The greater the efforts, the greater the resistance will be. When a student wishes to emulate a teacher, or some other significant individual, changes in speech will come naturally and imperceptibly. But when identity is challenged, characteristic aspects of speech will be reinforced rather than diminished.

8

Our Identity

Like a submerged rock in a narrow channel, a dire obstruction awaits anyone who tries to chart the course of language in human affairs—and that's the question of who's in charge. Who exactly has the thoughts, chooses the words to express those thoughts, and understands the words that express the thoughts of others?

There's a similar problem with vision. (It's the same problem really.) I glance through my window and see a bird. How do I see the bird? It can't be that my eyes send pictures back to the brain, because (1) they don't—any image is broken up and distributed to several parts of the brain—and (2) if the eyes did send pictures back to the brain, what is there inside the brain to look at them? Where's the "me?" If there's an eye inside the brain that looks at the inner pictures, how does that eye work? Is there another eye behind that eye that looks at the pictures? And another behind that eye? Once again, attributing something to the brain is no answer at all.

AN I FOR AN EYE

Suppose I were to read part of the previous paragraph aloud to you—"*If there's an eye inside the brain that looks at the inner pictures, how does that eye work? Is there another eye behind the eye that looks at the pictures?*" You might think that I'm saying "*If there's an I inside the brain that looks at the inner pictures, how does that I work? Is there another I behind the I that looks at the pictures?*" And it wouldn't make the slightest difference. It's the same philosophical conundrum.

THE CONUNDRUM

It's easy to deny that any problem exists. I can say something because I have learned how to talk, and you can understand what I say because you also have learned to talk. That's obvious, isn't it? But how exactly the trick is accomplished is an enigma that neither science nor philosophy has been able to explain despite hundreds of years of effort. I talk as if I have solved the problem, but really I am only offering a hypothesis (drawing on ideas of my own and those of many other people). I could be wrong. But then it is foolish to claim the last word on any topic—though there is no shortage of individuals always ready to do so.

Fine words. And there's the problem. Where have the words and thoughts I have just expressed come from? It's a very shallow answer to say "They came from *me. I* had those thoughts and *I* put them into words." It's equally shallow—and totally shunned in this book—to say "They came from my brain." Here are a few of the difficulties:

- Who is this *me* (or *I*)? It doesn't help to answer "*Me* is my body" because what is it about the body that is capable of generating these thoughts of *me?*

- Where does the idea of *me* come from? Where did I ever learn that I was me? Do animals have a similar sense of identity?

- What am I talking about when I say I understand what you are saying? What is this "understanding" that I claim to have? Who or what is this *I* that has the understanding? (Once again, it would be no answer to say it's the brain or some part of the brain. No one has ever seen *understanding* in the brain or known what to look for.)

- What is a thought? If it is words, what makes words come unbidden to us? (If the words are bidden, who bids them?) If thought isn't words, what is a nonverbal thought like? How can a nonverbal thought be converted into words? Who or what decides that the right words have been selected to express a thought?

Here's my proposal. The idea of *I* comes from language. I'll try to show how language by itself, with no help from any other parts of my body (or my brain), gives each of us the idea of *I*, of personal identity.

All of our ideas about thinking and reflecting also come from language. Language tells us—misleadingly—what we are doing and how we do it.

LANGUAGE DEVICES, INSIDE AND OUTSIDE THE BODY

The linguist Noam Chomsky used to talk about a language acquisition device, LAD, to explain language learning by infants. (Girls were supposed to have a language acquisition system, LAS.) More recently Chomsky has said that language is so unique that it should be considered a separate organ, like the stomach or the kidneys.

If there is indeed a separate and distinct language device in the body, then it should, in principle at least, be possible to imagine such a device operating outside the body, just as the transmission could be removed from the rest of an automobile and still be made to function independently.

So let's imagine a language device on a workbench rather than in the body. It could be a mechanical contrivance, or a combination of electronic hardware and software, or even a Frankensteinian brew of neurons and chemicals. We're not going so far as to *build* the machine, just to think about how it would work—what Einstein used to call a thought experiment. By moving our language device outside the body, we can insulate it from metaphysical influences of any kind, such as souls, inner selves, executives, or homunculi. This external language device has to be self-sufficient.

I also want to show that our language device, inside or outside the body, can function without any mystical process called *understanding*. Understanding is one of the many words language gives us that are perfectly suitable as descriptions but not as indicators of internal processes.

Our external language device must be capable of (1) producing outgoing sentences, and (2) responding to incoming sentences. We won't ask the device actually to *do* something when it receives incoming language—we won't call upon it to tie its shoelaces or take a jar from a shelf—because obviously it won't have that kind of capacity. We have removed all connections to other parts of a body. But we shall require it to demonstrate an appropriate reaction to incoming language by producing some acceptable outgoing language—like saying "I can't" or "What are you talking about?" if asked to tie its shoelaces. We could even put a bit of temperament into it, so that it might respond, "I can't do *that*, stupid!" (Hooking up the external language device so that it can produce sounds and "hear" incoming language can be regarded as a purely technical problem, not relevant to the operation of an actual or imagined device.)

Obviously, our external language device will have to be constructed from parts that will do the job we expect it to do—to receive and produce sentences. This prewiring will be the equivalent of the genetic preparedness of human infants for language—something that enables them to learn language in general without specifying details of the particular language that they will actually encounter and learn. The external device is just a way of thinking about the operation of the human device, without all the distractions of everything else supposed to be going on within the human skull.

To begin with, an external language device would need a supply of words and grammatical rules to work with. Where could it get those from? It doesn't have access to an actual human, so we'll say instead that it will have to get vocabulary and grammar by interacting with another external language device that already has language (much as an infant has access to the vocabulary and grammar of people around).

The experienced external language device transmits a message to our naive external language device, which doesn't have the slightest idea (metaphorically speaking) of what the experienced one is talking about. The term "message" is misleading but unavoidable. The word implies an intention on the part of the sender and an understanding on the part of the receiver. But external language devices are mechanical devices; they don't have intentions and they don't—as I'll explain shortly—have understanding. They just do what they do. It is difficult to find a neutral term to replace the loaded word *message*. The word *signal* is perhaps worse because it implies a message that is coded. The terms *information* and *data* might be appropriate in a technical sense, when they apply to uninterpreted events that do not necessarily have meaningful content, but that is not their popular use. So I must stay with the word message with the qualification that it should not be taken to mean someone is actually saying some*thing* to someone else.

Our external language device writes down—or otherwise records—the message it has received, let's say "How are you today?" The external language device also records any other messages it receives. We have built our external language device so that it can't sit still forever receiving messages without responding to them. So what can our external language device do? Its only option is to send back one of the messages it has already received.

The external language device has been asked "How are you today?" In turn it produces that message itself. When it does so it receives the response "I'm fine, thank you," which it duly records.

The next time the external language device receives the message "How are you today?" it will politely respond "I'm fine, thank you." It's not much, but it's a start. And note that this exchange doesn't involve any kind of *comprehension* in the sense of the feeling of understanding that we might expect from humans. External language devices are mechanical in their operation—but they manage to say the right kind of thing in the circumstances. They are indeed robots—though it might appear that they understand what they are doing.

Let's continue the demonstration, showing that even meaningful conversations can take place without understanding. Every time the external language device receives a message, it modifies itself to include what it has received. If it can respond, it responds. Otherwise it transmits something it has already received and modifies itself to include the new response.

Soon the external language device has built up a repertoire of statements it can make. It has also built up a repertoire of responses that it can make to messages. The two devices can hold conversations. To a human observer, these conversations would make sense, but to the external language devices they are simply exchanges of messages. There is nothing that might be called understanding, just an appropriate use of language. What does "appropriate" mean? It *fits*. It sounds like the kind of conversation one might come across in a movie or a book—or in "real life."

We could wire a little bit of technology to the external language device, just to make things more interesting, say red and green lights on the left and right sides, and a compass. Then when the external language device is asked, "Which of your side lights is on?" or "In which direction are you facing?" the device could give a sensible answer. This is all trivial stuff really—a beverage-dispensing machine could do as well. No "consciousness" is required. We could also wire in the little bit of temperament I referred to earlier. If we were to ask the same question twice, the external language device could respond, "Not again, blockhead"—provided the device had already encountered a tone and expression like that.

None of this may sound much like an infant learning to talk, but then we haven't given our external language device the environment the infant has. When someone says, "Here's a drink for you" to an infant, the infant can see the drink, and relate the proffered drink to the uttered words. We tend to associate such situations with "understanding"—it would be easy to say that the infant "understands" that the word *drink* is related to the offered drink. But what is such a concept of "understanding"—an actual state of affairs in the infant or merely a descriptive term that we use for such appropriate states of affairs? The fact that the infant says and responds to the word *drink* in appropriate ways doesn't mean that there's some mysterious "understanding" going on. We could make the external language device behave in exactly the same way without saying that understanding is taking place. External devices don't have feelings. Brains don't have feelings. People do.

PEOPLE WORDS AND PART WORDS

I am not saying that there is anything wrong with the word *understanding*—it's a useful (and comprehensible) word to use when we are talking about *people*. It is perfectly legitimate for me to express the hope that you will understand what I say, and equally legitimate for you to respond that you do (or don't) understand me. The word earns its keep in the language. But the word only applies at the level of people, to complete individuals. It doesn't apply to parts of people, in particular their brains. To say that the brain understands something is metaphorical at best and dangerously misleading. There is no part of the brain where understanding resides. What would such a part look like?

People words are words that apply to complete individuals—like thinking, hoping, feeling, joy, despair. *Part words* apply to outer and inner parts of people, like arms and legs, brains and kidneys, which can't be said to be thinking, hoping, feeling, and so forth. They are mechanisms. Mind is a people word. Brain is a part word. People have minds; brains don't. People understand and have other feelings, but brains and other body parts don't.

There is no part of the brain that understands—or misunderstands—any more than there is a part of us that feels happy, sad, anxious, eager, or crazy with desire. There is no part of the brain that feels pain (surgeons don't need to anesthetize the brain to perform surgery on it), which is usually (not always) felt in an affected limb or organ. Pain belongs exclusively to the individual who experiences it; its presence in another might be observed but not felt. We say, "I feel your pain"—but we don't.

ENVELOPING CONSTRUCTS

There's another new term and new concept that I have to introduce at this point. Some words obviously refer to observable parts of people (like arms, legs, ears, eyes, noses). But some words only refer to people as a whole—you can't point to a location for them.

Seeing and hearing are cases in point. We know that the eyes and the ears are involved in seeing and hearing—we can easily block either with our hands. But we can't say that our experience of seeing takes place in the eyes or hearing in the ears. The whole person does the seeing and hearing, and we can't point to a particular part of the body where the seeing and hearing are taking place.

If I kick a ball, I know and can see that my foot is involved. If I shake hands with you, I can see and feel which of my hands I am doing it with. But if I see *you*, which part of my body do I feel is doing this? I know, intellectually, that my eyes are involved. But I don't feel that my eyes are doing the seeing. Something greater than my eyes is seeing—something as substantial as *me*. I say, "I saw my daughter last night," not "My eyes saw my daughter last night." If I say I listened to a concert, I don't say, "My ears (or my brain) listened to a concert." I say that *I* did.

Whatever it is that is experiencing the seeing and hearing is much greater than the parts that I know are doing it. But this is odd. I can't say that my eyes and ears are doing the seeing and hearing, but I also can't say that my body as a whole is doing those things, the way my body as a whole might be feeling cold or tired. Obviously it is not. All I can say is that I feel it is me, as a whole, that is having these experiences, even though I can't point to a part of my body where the feeling is located, nor can I say that my body as a whole is having the relevant sensations. All I can say is that *I* have the feelings. And this *I* is what I now want to call an *enveloping construct.* The *I* that I talk and think about most of the time is neither a part of my body nor all of it, but rather something that surrounds and suffuses my body, that *envelops* it. No part of the body can claim it, but all of my body (and mind) is part of it.

Seeing and *hearing* are enveloping concepts—they are not done by our eyes and ears, but they are also not done by our body as a whole. They are done by some larger concept, which somehow envelops us, that includes our mind, body, feelings, values, and desires. *Self* is another enveloping concept. We can't find it in any particular part of the body, but it's not appropriate to say that our entire body somehow identifies itself as our *self.* We are enveloped in self—without being able to point to it in any way.

(As a complication, we are usually not aware of seeing or hearing, but of what we see and hear. I look out of my window at the moment at trees laced with snow. I'm not aware that I'm seeing them—I'm aware of what I see.)

When I say that you and I understand each other, I'm not referring to our bodies, but to something greater—our enveloping construct of ourselves.

WHAT THE LANGUAGE DEVICE NEEDS

Clearly, I haven't constructed an imaginary language device with the capacity of producing language as we know and use it. But language is incredibly complicated, and so is the human who produces and responds to language. If we really hoped to build an external language device capable of producing and responding to all the language that our human language device is capable of, we would have to build something as complex as a person. And I can't even imagine how that might be done. But we know that a language device can be constructed, because most of us have one. So we are not talking about something that is in principle impossible.

Even if a large part of the human ability to master language is built into humans at birth, in the genes, then it would still—in principle, of course—be logically possible to construct an external language device with similar properties by similar processes.

To emphasize the point I am making, the external language device, like our own language device, must be capable of doing everything concerned with language completely on its own. It doesn't need a control center, or an executive, to be in charge. It doesn't need "consciousness" or self-awareness. The external language device is a purely mechanical device. Ascribing an additional control function would only make the construction problem more complicated. In the same way, the human language device must operate without any kind of control system. An "executive" in charge of the human language device, or even just monitoring it, would also have to be specialized in language, a super language device in fact. So we must assume that the human language device is capable of managing its own affairs, without any mysterious process of "understanding." The language device simply does what it does, just like my imagined external language device.

WHAT THE LANGUAGE DEVICE DOESN'T NEED

There are some things an external language device doesn't need, for example, feelings of its own. The device can function without *feeling* that it understands, and it can be confused without *feeling* that it is confused. And the human language device is the same. It looks after language, but it doesn't have any feelings about what it does. The *feeling* of understanding or confusion is added by our emotions.

The external language device and human language device don't need a sense of self—not in the sense of "This is me doing this." The device just does what it does. The issue of "self" doesn't arise. The *language* within which the external language device and human language device operate makes a distinction between *me* and *you*, and includes a concept of *identity*. But these concepts are in the language that the devices encounter not in the devices themselves. The external language device might say, "This is me," but not because it has a sense of who it is, only because it is an appropriate thing to say. The idea of "self" is just another concept the language device manipulates without any feeling related to the concept itself. "Myself" is just an address.

One reason the language device doesn't need any feelings of self, of identity, or even of anxiety or confusion, is that such feelings are irrelevant to its operation. Our external language device doesn't need feelings to do its job—it is just a mechanical device, after all—and the same applies to the human language device. The external language device doesn't need any kind of consciousness to do its job—so the concept of *understanding* would be meaningless—and the human language device doesn't need any consciousness either. We are never aware that we are in the process of constructing something to say (though we are often aware of what we think we might say, because those thoughts are already in words, produced so silently that only we can hear them. That is "talking to ourselves.")

We may seem to be aware of the input and output of the human language device—we hear what someone is saying and hear our own reply. But that hearing doesn't mean that we understand what we are hearing before it gets to or from the language device. The understanding—or rather the appropriate manipulation of language—takes place *in* the language device. What would be the point of another language device in the vicinity of our ears, just to make sense of incoming language before it is passed on to the actual language device? Instead what we have when we hear ourselves or someone else talking is the *feeling* of understanding (or of confusion) that accompanies the operation of the language device.

WHERE FEELINGS COME FROM

Like the external language device, the human language device can continue to be regarded as an independent self-maintaining, self-controlling, and self-monitoring aspect of ourselves. Nevertheless our language device needs some access to other things we know and feel. Otherwise the language device would have nothing of a personal nature to talk about. So here's another conundrum. How can we have interaction with a system that is separate and independent?

Obviously we can say we feel cold, or worried, or eager. We can talk about things we see and things we hear. The language device may be a distinctive aspect of us, but it is not incommunicado. Unlike the external language device on the workshop bench, the human language device is wholly integrated with each individual. Or rather, the entire individual operates—in some contexts—as a language device. Language is not an add-on; it is original equipment. (I'm tempted to use the metaphor "factory installed," though I don't want to be misunderstood.) Language is naturally involved with everything we feel and do.

So where is *understanding*? The answer is nowhere. Understanding is a people word, a descriptive term applicable to a person as a whole, not a part of the person, or an external device. There is no *process* of understanding. When our language device produces or responds to language in a way that is appropriate, we might say the language device is understanding what it is doing, but that is just metaphorical talk. Feelings are not part of the language device. They are generated by an individual's emotions, which react to conditions affecting the individual as a whole.

Thus when the language device is functioning in an appropriate manner, emotional color may be added to give the *feeling* of understanding. Usually, of course, the understanding is not something we are aware of; it is the status quo and we take it for granted. But we are certainly aware when there is a *lack* of appropriate activity in the language device, when we get a feeling of being confused or uncertain; then emotions arise.

Our language device doesn't have feelings of confusion or uncertainty because the language device doesn't have emotions. But people can sense confusion and uncertainty in the language device, just as we can detect injury or uncertainty in other parts of the body, for example, if we stumble and stub a toe.

THE LANGUAGE DEVICE AND MEANING

The human language device is obviously a powerful mechanism. It enables us (as people) to feel we are making sense of language generated by the language devices of other people and to make statements that are understandable by other people (that are interpretable by their language devices).

Although the human language device has no sense—it is a purely mechanical device—it operates in a sphere of meaning. It acts and responds in accordance with the meaning of the language situation it is in, and it has to ascertain the meaning of new words that it encounters. The language device must be *sensitive* to meaning—without any understanding. How is that sensitivity achieved?

The answer is that the language device (and the external language device before it) organizes the meaning of words in relation to the meaning of other words. This may appear to be a completely circular assertion, and it is. But consider the case of any dictionary.

Dictionaries define words but only in terms of other words. For labeling purposes they may resort to pictures, giving an illustration of a bird as part of the meaning of the word *bird*. But usually the definition of words is given in terms of other words. What else can a dictionary do? Does that mean that a dictionary is a completely closed system and that definitions of all words are ultimately circular? (How is theft defined? As larceny. How is larceny defined? As theft. Making the definitions more complex doesn't escape the web of language.)

The only situation in which meaning is directly attached to words from something outside the body is in *labeling*—the attachment of names to objects, actions, or perceptible attributes. And labeling is barely a linguistic activity—labeling or identification could be achieved by using numbers, colors, or any kind of distinctive symbols. The most common method of identification these days is the bar code. But if you want to know what any label means—what the illustration or the number or the bar code stands for—then you are straight back into language again. A label may enable you to identify something as a tree or a bird, but language is needed to understand and explain what a tree or a bird is.

The richest understanding of words is indeed through the way they are related to other words. Ask someone what *perseveration* means, or *tergiversation*, or *antidisestablishmentarianism*, and they will explain in other words. Ask what the explanatory words mean, and they will respond with other words, until they find words that enable you to pin down the meaning of the target word. There is nothing unnatural about this—it is the way words work. As I pointed out earlier, language is a logical system. Word meanings triangulate with each other. Through structures of words, you can find meanings for words you haven't previously encountered and meanings that don't (yet) have a word attached.

Language can do a variety of things, from naming ships and solemnizing marriages to uttering threats and promises, but in every case, the *meaning* of the language that is employed can only be explained in other language (or in images of other kinds that in turn must be explained by language). Language is an entirely closed system, in people as in dictionaries.

The reason we are generally not aware of the circularity of language is that normally we are engaged in only a small part of it. The part of the labyrinth in which you roam may seem to lead to the world outside—but you are still in a labyrinth. A major difference between humans and all other creatures is that we are cocooned in a world of language, a world from which we cannot escape. We may think that language stands between us and the physical world, because we can use statements to accomplish ends or convey information about the physical world, but the meaning of language is tied up in itself, not in the world. Language to us is like water to a fish, something that is not normally explored or questioned.

(Language is a closed system like that other great logical structure, *mathematics*. We may make use of mathematics in making statements and accomplishing ends in the physical world, but the meaning of mathematics, even the meaning of $2 + 3 = 5$, can only be explained in mathematics. You can never get into mathematics through routes in the physical world, and you can never explain mathematics from outside the system.)

A related reason why we are usually unaware of the circularity of meaning in language is that we always *feel* that we are saying something that has some external reality. We feel we have pulled the bits of language we use out of the mass of the system and made something with independent status. But the bits of language that we use—whether brief assertions or three-volume novels—can't be regarded as separate from the entire mass of language. By themselves they would have no meaning. What makes any piece of language meaningful is the rest of language hovering always in the background.

This is how our language device (like the external language device) learns. It pursues meaning (though it has no concept of meaning itself) by locating new terms in the network of words it is already familiar with. (Psychologists have demonstrated that this is how children learn—they make a "fast mapping" of a possible meaning for a new word from the context it is in, usually getting close on the first try and achieving complete understanding by the sixth.) Our language device places new words in the network of semantic relations it has already established, and thereby locks new words in a meaningful context. The placement of new words may often result in the readjustment of the place of other words. In trying to find a logical place for new words, the language device finds and elaborates meaning (though it doesn't *sense* meaning itself because it has no sense).

INSIDE THE LANGUAGE DEVICE

A large part of human thought involves words—often our thought is entirely a matter of words—which means that the language device is the place where most of our thinking takes place. When we think we are thinking, or have been thinking, it is usually our language device that is involved. The language device provides us with the basis for feeling that we are intelligent, creative, language-using individuals. The language device does the work, and the entire person takes the credit.

Language is an essential aspect of categorization (particularly noticeable in hierarchical categorization), so there has to be a category component within the language device. If a categorizing system that needed constant access to language existed outside the language device, then it would require a language device of its own, an unnecessary redundancy.

The same considerations apply to reasoning. It is difficult to imagine how an independent reasoning system might function with no content of its own, or with content that redundantly replicates content elsewhere. It is again much more reasonable to expect human language to have its own embedded reasoning processes.

One significant function of the language device is often said to be the communication of thoughts (or ideas) from one person to another. This gets by as person language, but it doesn't describe what the language device is doing. Language devices exchange meanings—without any awareness, of course, of what they are doing. One language device transmits to another language device, which makes an appropriate response. This is mechanical.

ACHIEVEMENTS OF THE HUMAN LANGUAGE DEVICE

So our language device has a vocabulary, a grammar for putting words together, numerous conventions for producing the appropriate words at the relevant time, and the power of reasoning. What else can this magnificent mechanism accomplish?

- The language device gives us the idea of *identity*. It doesn't understand the word, but it is able to use it appropriately (in terms of other words). We have the feeling of understanding the term, and it be-

comes applied to ourselves. We respond emotionally when our identity is modified, challenged, or uncertain. Identity is not the same as
self. Self is *me*, passive, primitive, and doesn't need language. It is a
genetic gift. *I* involves meaning and comes from language.

- The language device is the difference between *automaticity* (habit-
ual or reflex behavior) and *attention* (vigilance). When we drive a
car, we are usually unaware of the hand and foot movements that
we make and of where our eyes are directed. We decelerate before
we reach the stop sign without having to say to ourselves, "There's
a stop sign; I should decelerate." All of this is "automatic" activity.
When we "pay attention," we use words to describe the situation
we are in and what we are doing.

- What goes on in the language device becomes regarded as
thought—*our* thought. The language device doesn't have
thoughts, but we feel that *we* do, as individuals, always with emotional color.

- The language device coordinates behavior. We read a recipe and
our eyes and hands are recruited to make the cake. Someone says,
"Look," and we look.

- The language device is where free will is exercised, where moral
choices are made. It is the only part of us that has access to the idea
of morality.

- The language device opens us to the influence of language. The language device doesn't have all the powers I have listed in itself; the
powers come from the *language* that the language device has access
to. All of the noble concepts behind our ideas of right and wrong, the
good, beauty, truth, fairness, and the meaning of life itself, are available in the abstract calculus of language. The language device ex-
plores these concepts. Love, charity, altruism, and all our finer
feelings may have a genetic basis, but they are honed by language.

- The language device is *us*—the basis of our independence, our morality, our laws and our politics, our learning, our curiosity, our exploring, our will.

The idea of a language device that operates without conscious control
doesn't entail that we have no self-control, no will, or no power to exer-

cise good impulses and restrain bad ones. All that control exists—within the language device. It is in the language device that our morality lies. The idea of a language device explains how we can review our behavior and decide what is appropriate and what is inappropriate for us to do. It doesn't mean we don't have a soul. The language device can create the idea of a soul and establish moral ideals that we (the language device again) can aim for. Increasing the number of entities that might control our behavior and beliefs (like souls, inner executives, and various "selves") doesn't explain anything—it leaves more to explain. Because the language device contains all our knowledge (all knowledge that can be put into words), what better or more likely place for decisions to be made and finer feelings (like fine words) expressed.

Pinker (2002) discusses how much of our behavior is genetically determined—but notes that these behaviors are frequently paired in incompatible or contrasting ways, so that there might be a gene for aggression but another gene for empathy. The alternatives make it possible for people to choose or reject particular kinds of behavior, with language (I argue) playing a particular role in our making a decision.

Once again, I reiterate that my purpose in all this discussion is to show that the human language device must and does operate without any mystical function called *understanding*. Understanding is a descriptive word applied to people as a whole; it's not a process that is a part of any one of us.

RESIDUAL ENIGMAS

But we are still left with a couple of riddles.

The first riddle regards this *self*, this *I*, that I have been talking about. Where does the idea of *I* come from? There are two tempting quick answers. The first is to say that we know we have a body that we inhabit, and we call that body "I" (or as appropriate, "me," when we hear other people using those words to refer to themselves). The second quick answer is a kind of mirror image of the first, except instead of relating the body that we know we have to the words that we hear, we hear the words (used by other people) and relate them to ourselves. The second quick answer suggests that we wouldn't get the idea of "I" if it weren't for language. Both quick answers are unsatisfactory because they take for granted that we have an awareness of being a person, of having not just a body, but thoughts that are generated by a mind, that we know belongs to *us*.

This leads to the second riddle. All this discussion of how we relate words like *I*, *me*, and *mine* to our body depends on our being conscious. We wouldn't have any understanding of our body or of language if we didn't have consciousness. That is the essential difference between an external language device and the human language device. An external device would need no access to a mind (it has nothing to talk about, if you like) while human language can only function in a conscious mind. But what is consciousness?

It is not enough, in an inquiry of this kind, to say that everyone knows what consciousness is. That may be true—*but what is it*? We can say what it is like to be walking, or running, or breathing, but we can't say what it is like to be conscious. Consciousness isn't something that we *do*, like walking, running, and so on. It's an enveloping construct. Consciousness just *is*, like seeing or hearing. Except we can say how seeing and hearing are done—we open the eyes, direct the gaze, focus attention, and so forth—but we can't say how consciousness is done. Neuroscientists have identified particular areas of the brain that seem to be involved in consciousness, in the sense that consciousness suffers if these areas are damaged. But these neural identifications give no clue as to what consciousness is or how is it done.

These may not even be two riddles but just one. If we could understand consciousness, then the feeling of *self* would be clear. And if we could understand how we achieve the feeling of selfhood, then there might be nothing left to ask about consciousness.

These are some of the issues to be confronted in the next chapter.

SUMMARY AND IMPLICATIONS FOR EDUCATORS

Personal identity is not something that we find by looking at ourselves in the mirror, nor is it given to us by the efforts and opinions of others. Identity is constructed from the way others influence the way we behave and see ourselves. We learn from the company we keep, and the greatest learning is generated by our perception of the way other people see us. We expect to be like our friends and other close acquaintances—and expect to be different from those with whom we don't affiliate.

Students won't be like their teachers unless they want to be like their teachers. If they don't want this identification, they will resist every effort to change the way they are and behave in forthright ways to assert their own individuality. The most teachers can hope to achieve is the most they can themselves offer to students who are essentially different people from them—mutual respect.

9

Our Consciousness

What is the role of consciousness in all this? It's easy to feel that we are in complete charge of our language, our movements, and most of the other things in which we are involved, and that consciousness allows us to exercise that control. We feel that consciousness is what distinguishes people from machines. Machines just function, but people are aware that they function.

Consciousness is a complex issue for two reasons. The first reason is that it is difficult to say what consciousness is. The second reason is that researchers have been unable to locate a physical location or process of consciousness in the brain. They know that if certain parts of the brain are damaged or incapacitated in some way, consciousness disappears. Anesthetics also bring that condition about. But this still doesn't tell researchers what consciousness is, or even how it is produced or directed by the brain. In recent years, explaining consciousness has become more the concern of philosophers than of neuroscientists and physiologists—suggesting that the problem might be more a matter of language and clarity of thought than of explaining brain structures.

Some philosophers have proposed that there is no such thing as consciousness—that it is just a concept in language that has no physical reality. Others suggest that we have not just one kind of consciousness but two, one looking out and one looking in. The two-consciousnesses proposal is related to old philosophical conundrums of how we know our own thoughts or that other people think the way we do.

I'm inclined to agree that there's no physical reality, or physical substance, to consciousness—but it exists; it is part of us. I don't see that any aspect of consciousness has access to whatever might be going on inside ourselves, in our body or that part of the body we call our mind. We can only be aware of ourselves from the outside, from the same perspective that we are aware of other people. We are aware of ourselves talking, just as we are aware of other people talking, as something taking place in the world, not in ourselves. Even if we talk silently, "to ourselves," it is still an external activity that we can hear ourselves engaged in. Even when we think we have access to our own thoughts, we are only listening to the voice we hear when we talk to ourselves, just as we can see "visual images" that don't physically exist inside us.

Some people think that consciousness is the same thing as awareness—and the two words may be synonymous in some contexts. But as a general distinction, awareness is only of the here and now—I am aware of what I see, hear, taste, feel, and touch at this moment. But consciousness can include the past and the future—it embraces the imagination.

WHAT CONSCIOUSNESS DOES

Consciousness can be regarded basically as a replay device. It enables us to have an experience more than once. Simple awareness enables us to respond to a situation, the way animals and some machines do (using the term *awareness* simply to indicate sensitivity and responsiveness to surroundings). But awareness is chained to what is happening right now, the focus of our attention. Perhaps the reason stalking animals gaze at their prey so intently is that they don't have the consciousness to retain an image of their situation if they glance elsewhere.

Consciousness of a situation enables us to reflect upon it. It provides the possibility of evaluating present and past experiences. Our past experiences become more than history; they become something we can think about critically and often pleasurably. Consciousness brings our past into our present. It presents the alternative to a memory store.

We can not only reflect on what was, we can consider what might have been. Few animals seem able to do this and then only in a rudimentary fashion. Humans can reflect not only on what might have happened in the past (but didn't) but also on what might happen in the future. Consciousness, in other words, makes imagination possible. Imagination is the power we have to generate experiences of what is *not* actually happening—experiences that we can talk about and write about as if they really took place in the world or in a medium like film and television.

Awareness exists only for aspects of physical activity that are observable, that manifest themselves in the world at large. Some parts of our body function in the absence of awareness, for example, digestion, the circulation of blood, and breathing. These activities continue even if we are unconscious. We are only conscious of what we can perceive ourselves doing—things that we can also perceive other people doing (or suffering). We are aware of what we say and hear, and of what we see, and with consciousness can reflect upon both. Without consciousness, we have neither language nor imagination.

This analysis gives us clues to the nature of consciousness. It is not a searchlight peering into every nook and cranny of the body, but rather it is a working partner of our senses. Consciousness frees vision and hearing from the constraints of the present and permits access to the past and to possible futures. We can talk of people having powerful visual imaginations or auditory imaginations—the imagination becomes a working part of perception.

Machines may evaluate input to determine appropriate responses; they can branch from one possible reaction to another, but they can't experience how the environment might react to different responses because they have no possibility of reruns; they have no imagination. Even if we give them reruns of experience, they have no way of evaluating them beyond a simple reaction, like the on–off of a thermostat.

WHAT ARE WE CONSCIOUS OF?

At first glance it might seem that we are conscious of everything going on around us —everything we are looking at or listening to, plus smells, tastes, and tactile experiences. As I have just indicated, we are conscious of everything we can perceive.

But consciousness is also limited by the limitations of perception. We can't sense anything that happens beyond the visual spectrum, in the infrared and ultraviolet regions, nor can we sense anything outside a narrow acoustic range, like the high pitches audible to dogs. There are also things that we have no sense of at all, like changes in pressure due to movements of objects around us, although this feat is accomplished by the lateral line organs of fish and many other creatures. Since we have no sense of anything outside the range of our perceptual abilities, these domains of possible experience can't enter into our consciousness. These are limits on consciousness.

On the other hand, we can put a great deal into our consciousness that was never part of our senses—the infilling role of the imagination, the *feeling* that we can see and hear more than we actually do. Research may show that we can see only a few words of the page we are looking at, but we feel we see everything. This may be a partial effect of peripheral vision—we have a general image extending beyond what we can perceive in detail—but our feeling that we see much more goes beyond imagination. We don't imagine we see more words on the page; if we did, we could imagine what they are. Instead we are conscious of the existence of more than we can perceive in detail.

Another aspect of consciousness going beyond the range of our senses is our empathetic relationship with others—we respond to their feelings, their states of mind, even if we can't point to the evidence that gives rise to our intuitions (and even if we don't personally know the individual whose feelings we intuit).

Part of the "everything going on around us" of which we are conscious includes, of course, our own body. We are aware of our limbs, of our movements, of feelings like hunger and fear, of emotional states, and of various aches and pains. Many of these conscious experiences seem to be coming from inside us, but they must fall into the category of external events. We have no direct access to anything going on inside the body, but for some of the body's internal activities (not all), feelings are projected outside, to this mysterious construction we call our "self."

CONSCIOUSNESS IS NOT IMMEDIATE

Consciousness of pain is an aftereffect. When we stub our toe or cut our finger, we withdraw our foot or hand from the damaging situation before we feel the pain. The protective movement is one of several physical responses (reflexes) organized in the spinal cord, which nerve impulses from the damaged part reach first. But the feeling arises after the damaged condition has been attended to. So it is not the pain that makes us move ourselves away from a threatening situation. Damage control is initiated by the spinal cord, and the pain alert is a belated response. Once again we are not conscious of the process (in the spinal cord) but of the end product, the feeling of pain.

In fact, all consciousness is delayed. One of the oldest and best established findings in experimental psychology is that we are never immediately conscious of anything. It takes about a fifth of a second for us to be aware of a sudden sound or a flash of light—as I discussed in chapter 4, under the heading of Limits to Perception.

Consciousness of bodily events can be seen as just another aspect of access to external conditions—we are only conscious of the exterior of our body or of what is projected to the exterior of our body. I am aware of my leg moving if I kick a ball but not of the mental or muscular logistics that went into the kick. Once again, everything is circular. We may be conscious only of external events (plus imagined events), but our experience of external objects and events—of "the world" around us—comes only by courtesy of our senses.

CONSCIOUSNESS AND THE SELF

Consciousness can also be regarded as the means by which our awareness of various and independent projections of physical and bodily activities, like hearing and sight, is put together into a coherent whole. With awareness but no consciousness (if we could imagine such a condition), we would simply be a conglomeration of parts—the head hurts, the foot is sore, the stomach aches. But consciousness pulls it all together into a *person*, an identity.

"Where is the *self*? Who is the *we*?" Language tells us it is all of us, our entire body and all our thoughts and feelings. Physically, the self is the generalized consciousness of specific perceptual activities plus large amounts of infilling provided by imagination. We think we are aware of much more than we actually are. Perception is more imagination than fact. We think we see everything in front of our eyes, but research shows that we see only a small part of it. You may feel you can see the entire page you are looking at right now, but close your eyes and say what you could see, and you will find it was only a few letters or words (p. 37).

Imagination fills in gaps, provides missing information, and generally enhances our feelings of power and awareness.

So where is our consciousness located, and where is our sense of self? We shouldn't expect to find them anywhere in the body, because they are ideas, not structures or processes. They are projections, not properties. Consciousness embraces my entire body, not one part of it, and the self claims the same territory.

What is the scientific answer to the conundrums of consciousness and self? There isn't one. Some researchers try to explain consciousness away, saying it's an illusion. But it's a remarkably universal illusion; it seems that everyone has it—even the philosophers who say it doesn't exist. Some have argued that consciousness and the self exist, but we don't have the kind of brain that can comprehend them. Just as the unaided visual system can't see infrared and the auditory system can't detect high pitches audible to dogs, so—by analogy—our intellect isn't equipped to penetrate mysteries of consciousness and self. The heightening (or calming) of consciousness that is supposed to occur as a result of certain meditational, biofeedback, or pharmacological interventions is a heightening (or calming) of all our senses.

One thing is clear. We all as individuals have a strong sense of our own consciousness and selfhood. Only sleep and anesthesia can take those feelings away from us. We might come around from surgery or a blow on the head asking "Where am I?" or "What happened?" but never "Who am I?" (unless we are suffering from a severe brain dysfunction). From a practical, pragmatic point of view we just have to accept our own awareness of the world and of ourselves, and we must grant that awareness to others. This makes consciousness no different from the experience of living, which I think is the case.

SO WHAT IS CONSCIOUSNESS?

Consciousness exists—but I can only describe it as I can see it manifested in others and in language. I can see you behaving in ways that I would call conscious—you are responding to your surroundings and to yourself. You appear to be engaging in fantasies (you can describe them). You don't appear to be a machine or a zombie. And since everything you do makes me believe you have this mysterious thing called consciousness, then I assume I have consciousness myself—the reflective flip to which I've referred.

Thus consciousness is not an inner feeling at all. I don't know consciousness as a personal experience, which I then attribute to other people. I detect what I call consciousness in you, simply because you seem to be aware of what you are doing, and I assume I have this consciousness myself.

This is my solution to the "other minds" problem. I don't have a special sense of having a mind of my own, and therefore attribute a mind to everyone else. I see everyone else behaving in ways that lead me to conclude they have something called a mind, and attribute the same faculty to myself.

Although I believe you (like everyone else) are conscious, I don't see your consciousness as restricted to any part of you. I can see that you look with your eyes, hear with your ears, and kick a ball with your feet. But I don't see where you are conscious. It is an attribute in which you seem to be enveloped.

Therefore, I see my own consciousness as something that envelops me. I no longer have to ask where consciousness comes from, because it is not a specific part of me or of you. Everything about the way you are behaving leads me to think that you are conscious—and I relate the same attribute to myself. Consciousness is a concept introduced to me through language. But it is not something I find in myself. I sum up what I see in you as an enveloping consciousness, and therefore think I have the same myself.

And how do we know that we have a self, that we are our selves? This is again a consequence of the reflective flip. We find words to characterize and explain the behavior of others and then reflect them onto—and into—ourselves. We don't have to provide a rationale for this—language makes the case for us, so we don't bother.

I remember my grandfather posing an old conundrum to me when I was a child. Two men are in a room. One has a speck of dirt on his nose; the other doesn't. The man without a speck rubs his nose. The man with the speck doesn't. Why? The answer is the reflective flip.

SUMMARY AND IMPLICATIONS FOR EDUCATORS

Consciousness allows our perceptual systems access to the past (memory) and to possible futures (prediction); it allows the imagination to become a working part of perception.

Students whose imaginations are not locked into whatever they are expected to learn can't be expected to succeed. They will literally lack consciousness of whatever the teacher is trying to impart—and unconscious people don't learn.

10

Our Technology

I should say what I mean by technology, and why I include institutions—like government, the legal system, and education—and also science, under the heading of technology.

My dictionary defines *technology* as the practical application of knowledge, which is fine as far as it goes. I shall expand the definition and regard technology as anything that amplifies natural human abilities. We have telescopes and microscopes that extend vision, telephones that extend speech and hearing, television to project images, and computers to facilitate thought. Other devices magnify our strength, our reach, and the speed at which we can move ourselves and other objects. Institutions extend our capacity to work together (not always productively, of course). A multitude of scientific instruments extend our ability to examine and understand the world, and another multitude of scientific processes extend the ways in which we can act upon the world and modify it. There seems to be no end to technology. A lot of technology simply serves other technology, the way the technology of software has no function except to be part of other technology. *Bureaucracies* are technologies that serve institutions. The hierarchy of technologies is a topic that I shall come back to—but the end point of all technology is its interaction with people.

The main reason for wanting to include institutions under the heading of technology is my own convenience. One can make an argument that they are technology, in the sense that people have created institutions that now have a life of their own. If I separate technology and institutions as subjects, I would have to repeat myself by saying mostly the same kinds of things about both. The same considerations apply to science, another topic which I might seem to ignore but which follows the same kind of existence as technology and institutions. All are artificial constructs that serve human beings, superficially at any rate, but that are also served by us. Institutions and science have the permanence of other kinds of technology. It is always possible for technology, including institutions and science, to be "improved" (a term I'll explain), but this usually takes place to increase the efficiency of the system rather than to meet human expectations or desires. It is difficult to halt technology, including institutions and science, or to deflect it in the direction that individuals might prefer. Usually, technology makes greater demands on people than people make on technology.

There may be arguments about how broadly I use the word technology, and whether institutions and science should be separate categories. But this is not a book about definitions; it is concerned with the whole range of systems and devices that have been added to the natural world and that impinge upon human possibilities in various ways. I want to project my inquiry about technology—the organization and reorganization of human abilities—into every corner of the topic. I don't mind if some people want to argue that some of the things I talk about are not literally technology and, specifically, that institutions and science are a different kind of thing from technology, because I don't want to argue about "what words mean." I am more concerned that the points I make are understandable and have no objection to reader reservations that references to technology should sometimes be regarded as references to "technology, institutions, science, and other systems." The important thing on both sides is to achieve mutual understanding.

THE EVOLUTION OF TECHNOLOGY

Why has technology developed over the centuries in the way that it has? Why do we have television and computers today while a century ago we did not?

It can't be said that people felt no need for these things in the past. Technology creates its own necessity; people wanted television and computers when that technology became available. A better explanation for the absence a century ago of television and computers (and refrigerators, jet airplanes, and magnetic resonance imaging) is that technology hadn't advanced to the point where those possibilities were feasible. With the development of the cathode ray tube and the transistor, the rapid evolution of television and computers began, an evolution that is still progressing rapidly.

Rather than people deciding the ways in which they want technology to develop, technology evolves in ways that it itself determines. People merely respond to what technology suggests to them. Technology controls itself.

When I use terms like "determines," " suggests," and "controls," it may seem that I am personifying technology, even that I am giving it a mind and a will. This is not the intention. Technology does *not* have a mind of its own (yet). Even when it acts as an artificial brain, examining evidence and making choices, it does not have a will. Technology is not alive, even if it can reproduce itself and behave in what are considered brain-like ways. Technology is not in our genes and can't therefore make a difference to human evolution (unless it brings an end to human reproduction).

Technology is passive and inanimate. But passive and inanimate objects continually influence human behavior. A dark cloud determines that I shall not venture far from my home today. A windmill suggests to me that I would enjoy a visit to Holland. A rock fall diverts the traffic on a highway. We respond to technology in the way we can respond to all objects, animate and inanimate. When I assert that technology dictates its own evolution, I don't mean that it seizes us by the arm—only by our constructive mind. As a whole, technology is a self-regulating system. It is always sensitive to changes in external and internal conditions, and it always moves toward maximized efficiency.

A good analogy for the self-maintenance of technology might be the human body itself. The body always responds to disequilibrium and stresses, inside and out. If one vein is blocked by a blood clot, other veins take over to compensate, not because of the "wisdom of the body"—that is a picturesque but inaccurate figure of speech—but because our body is an adaptive and self-regulatory system. To the extent that circumstances allow it, the body always responds to inner and outer conditions in ways that will maintain and even improve its efficiency.

The body is a homeostatic device—it will always adapt to maintain an equilibrium, to ensure stable growth. Technology is the same.

THE ORIGINS OF TECHNOLOGY

Every aspect of technology begins with an insight, a discovery rather than an invention. Technology is a consequence of understanding, of realization. Geniuses *see* connections and possibilities.

Technology may have begun with fire—the realization that the source of warmth could be deliberately transferred and controlled. Or with tools—the realization that a rock could be a pounding instrument and that a more convenient pounding instrument could be fabricated. Or with the realization that a floating log could carry a person, and a hollowed out log could do it even better. Always, the development was the result of a discovery rather than an invention.

What was the role of the stars? Ancient people employed the nightly pageant of the stars as a clock, calendar, and compass, and a few still do today. Nothing was invented for hundreds of years, until the development of practical implements like plows and telescopes. The realization that the slowly changing patterns in the night sky could be of service in human affairs produced a technology without the construction of anything more substantial than mental models.

Few inventions have been solitary events. Fire, cooking, weapons, agriculture, and alchemy seem to have been discovered independently, at different times, in different part of the world, spurred by environmental demands and possibilities.

Why does technology change? Always because efficiency can be increased. New uses are found for technology that already exists, and existing technology is improved to increase economy and utility. The development always moves from what is to what would be better. Inefficient technology is replaced or superseded.

It could be argued that all of these changes are brought about by people wanting to produce a more economical or more useful technology. But these ideas of improvement don't come from nowhere. They don't spring from barren ground. Improvements and new developments always come from what exists already. Existing technology *tells us* (in its passive, inanimate, yet eloquent way) how the improvements could be made.

There's a symbiotic relationship between people and technology. People develop and improve technology, but only within the parameters suggested by technology itself. There would be no development of technology without people (not so far, as least). But we would never have had the technology that exists today without the technology that existed yesterday.

Here's an abbreviated table for the evolution of ships:

- A floating log
- Two logs tied together
- Multiple pieces of wood tied together
- Structures built on the deck
- Rudders and oars added
- Ships become weapons of war as well as means of transportation
- A sail added
- Skilled design and construction techniques developed
- Shipbuilding becomes an industry
- All aspects of ships improved, from nails to ropes
- Metal replaces wood
- Engines replace sails
- Propellers replace paddle wheels
- Ships increase in size and structure for specialized purposes.

All of the developments in the preceding table came from what existed before. Nothing was without antecedents. Other technologies developed simply because they were demanded by the technology of ships. They include:

- Jetties
- Harbors
- Ports
- Ancillary vessels (tugs, barges)
- Weapons (torpedoes)
- Cranes and other equipment
- Shipyards

- Containers
- Warehouses
- Special provisioning
- Navigational systems
- Parts and other supplies
- Dry docks
- Offices
- Communication systems
- Roads
- Regulations
- Laws
- Special software
- Satellites (the Global Positioning System)

and each of those just listed spawned other new sets of technologies that were required for their efficient operation.

ESTABLISHING A BASELINE

Consider again stages of my illustrative table of the evolution of ships, abbreviated even further:

- Multiple pieces of wood tied together
- Structures built on the deck
- Rudders and oars added
- Metal replaces wood
- Engines replace sails
- Propellers replace paddle wheels

At each stage of this evolution of ships, people who were living at the time thought the technology that they had was *modern*, the latest word. The latest floating objects were the obvious way floating objects ought to be. A lumbering wooden vessel with an untidy array of sails and ropes was state of the art. Anything prior to the present was antiquated, a curiosity. But anything that might happen in the future was unimaginable. The way things were was the way things were supposed to be.

The state that the evolution of ships had reached was the baseline for all people born at that time who made the acquaintance of ships. There was nothing unnatural about a lumbering wooden vessel with an array of sails and ropes; it was a part of the way the world had to be. It was taken for granted. This was not the same baseline that people had a hundred years previously nor what people would have a hundred years later. The 18th century sailor would be lost on today's container ship. "Modern" is a relative term, not to the individual but to the time in which the individual is born. But it is also relative to the baselines and ceilings of people living at that time.

To the young, modern is not a relative adjective at all; it is synonymous with contemporary. It is close to their baseline idea of the necessary structure of the world. But to someone whose baseline was established a generation or more earlier, modern might well be synonymous with radical, if not revolutionary, difficult to understand and to adapt to.

As technological development moves further away from a person's baseline construction of the world, it moves closer to the ceiling of comprehensibility. The progression from one form of technology to another—say from dialing numbers to punching keys on telephones—is easily accomplished by someone close to the baseline but not for someone closer to the ceiling. This is not a matter of age but of the rate at which new technology develops. The further technology gets from what we take for granted, from our baseline view of the world, the more difficult it is for us to adjust to innovation.

Innovation is more acceptable to the young than to the old. This is common wisdom. The passage of time moves everyone from a baseline, where every experience is regarded as natural, the way things have to be, toward a ceiling, where every new experience becomes an intrusion. This applies to more than hardware—look at responses at different ages to "modern" art and music. The philosopher of progress, Ronald Wright, believes that we reach a ceiling for all kinds of new experience by the age of 50.

HOW TECHNOLOGY IMPROVES ITSELF

What do I mean by "improve"? Become more efficient. What do I mean by efficient? To do what is done more effectively and more economically. Who decides what is more effective and more economical? People.

Therefore, people are responsible for improvement in technology. Right? Wrong. People make the decisions, but they don't do so by sitting as impartial judges. They are always influenced. What influences them? The current state of technology and an improvement that suggests itself, as indicated by the technology. People may choose between alternative developments in technology (or between doing something and doing nothing), but the alternatives are always made obvious by the technology. And such is the power that technology has over people; people (in general) always choose to improve technology rather than leave it as it is.

Why can we not just leave technology the way it is? Let's look at the power that technology has over people a little more closely.

THE DOMINANCE OF TECHNOLOGY

There are two main reasons why technology holds sway. The first, which applies especially at the beginning of any aspect of technology, including institutions, is that it extends human powers. Realizing that one can sit on a floating log to get from one side of a river to the other is an extension of personal power. The discovery that a piece of glass can magnify the image of whatever is on the other side is another extension of human power. So is the insight, the discovery, that a device at each end of a piece of wire can project a voice from one room to another. Once any human ability is amplified, there is no desire to restrict it again.

The technology that extends our abilities to see, reach, feel, examine, and communicate becomes part of ourselves—just as a pencil becomes part of our hand. We don't make notes with our fingers, but with the point of the pencil that extends beyond our fingers. "Us"—our feeling of where our body is—extends beyond ourselves. The garments that we happen to be wearing are part of us—we try not to let them touch other people's garments as we walk through a crowded mall or stand in an elevator. We flinch when someone else's attempt to park a car gets dangerously close to our vehicle. Our body writhes as we try to project a trajectory on the bowling ball we have just sent down the alley. We assimilate into ourselves any part of our environment that we feel to be relevant to ourselves. (And committees and other institutions become part of the way we think. We think that people become part of the institutions they serve, but the institutions become part of the people who serve them.)

So the technology that is useful to us becomes part of us. We can't ignore it because it is inside us. It has become us, and we respond to it as we respond to any other physical or mental feeling that is generated inside ourselves.

But the second, more important reason why technology has such a hold over our lives is that *it is there*. It exists as a significant part of the external landscape. We can neither dislodge nor ignore it. It is a fully functioning part of our environment when we are born, as natural and inevitable in our minds as the earth and the sky. It becomes part of our baseline for constructing a world—a substantial and influential part in most people's minds.

Technology is a dominant part of everyone's life even if we try to turn our backs on it. We may decide not to acquire a car, but other people's cars are all around us and will not go away. We may resolve never to ride in vehicles that burn carbon fuels—but we had better look out for them when we cross the road. And the roads themselves, the super highways that slice through our cities, and the interchanges, and the noise, pollution, inconvenience, and injury that they bring, will not go away, no matter how much individuals may deplore them. You may not care for air travel, but you can't ignore the presence of planes in the sky, their noise, and the airports that impede your way as you try to drive, walk, or cycle from one part of the countryside to another. Technology rules.

Not only can you not ignore technology, you can't stop other people from using it and developing it. In general, the people who need, use, or support technology have more political clout than the people who don't. Some aspects of technological development are repugnant to many people, even to some governments, for example, in genetic engineering, reproductive processes, and cloning. But even if a vast majority of people reject some form of technology, someone, somewhere, will take the plunge and make use of it. Why will some people blatantly disregard the deepest convictions of many others? Not necessarily for money or for power, though their aims are usually characterized in this way. They do it because they can't resist the perceived improvement in technology.

The means are there, let's use them. Potential developments in technology do not need to appeal to everyone for the development—the "advance"—to be made. A few people are highly attracted—let us say that they are highly susceptible to the enchantment of the new technology—and they readily succumb.

Once again, I am awash in anthropomorphic language, not only saying that technology determines, suggests, and controls, but also that it attracts and enchants. I am talking as if technology has a mind of its own, as if it were a living organism. But then technology affects us as if it were a living organism with a mind of its own. Rather than objecting that it doesn't, because only human beings have minds, let's grant that anything that behaves as if it had a mind might just as well be granted a mind—albeit a qualitatively different kind of mind from ours—so that we can get on with reflecting about the consequences of its existence.

We grant other people reflective minds, self-interest, and intentions, because they behave in the way we would expect them to behave if they really did have reflective minds, self-interest, and intentions: the reflective flip. Technology, as a whole, exhibits similar characteristics.

Technology is not simply something that exists in the world outside ourselves. It has started to move into our minds and will do so more and more as the space between the baseline and the ceiling of our grasp of new technology lessens. We have already examined one instance of a technology moving into our minds, making "us" feel that its properties and functions are our own. And this is language. Technology is as silently pervasive, influential, dominant, and taken for granted in our lives as language.

SUMMARY AND IMPLICATIONS FOR EDUCATORS

Technology exists independently of the people who use it (which means all of us), even of those people who help modify and develop new technology. The contribution any individual can make to moving technology forward is relatively minimal, like one person trying to push an ocean liner from a dock.

For students, technology is like the weather: something that exists, that can be taken advantage of, but that is fundamentally beyond individual control. Students find technology fascinating—provided no one tries to teach them *about* it. Teachers shouldn't stand between students and technology, but they shouldn't employ technology to force learning on their students. Technology can be invaluable to teachers hoping to expand the horizons of their students, but like every other aspect of learning, it can't be achieved without the collaboration, the imaginative involvement, of the learner.

11

Ourselves

You might feel that after all the thousands of words in all the previous chapters, I still haven't caught the essence of what it means to be a person, to be ourselves. We are molded by language and by technology. But these do not make us individuals.

What have I left out?

One thing that makes us individuals, of course, is our physical appearance, and our personal mannerisms. No two people are completely alike, not even identical twins.

Not so conspicuous but equally distinguishing are our habits, what we do and how we do it, from organizing a day to using implements for eating.

But none of these characteristics, not even all of them grouped together, could be said to define a person.

What makes the difference is something truly personal that I alluded to in chapter 5—our hopes, fears, and desires.

HOPES, FEARS, AND DESIRES

The Greek writer Nikos Kazantzakis had a personal motto that he carried with him throughout life and had carved on his gravestone. I even have a t-shirt with the motto on it in Greek, because I greatly admire Kazantzakis. But I don't believe his motto. It says:

I hope for nothing, I fear nothing, I am free.

This was false for Kazantzakis himself. He was also a politician, and all politicians have hopes and fears, hopes that they will be reelected and fears that they won't.

Hoping for nothing and fearing nothing is not even my definition of freedom. It sounds like death. Hoping and fearing—and desiring—is the essence of freedom. It is also what makes us who we are.

Know someone's hopes, fears, and desires, and you know that person. If you don't know their hopes, fears, and desires, you can't say you know the person.

Everything I have talked about concerning our powers, limitations, knowledge, and stupidities is not enough to make a person. It applies to all of us. What makes people distinguishable from each other, and enables us to distinguish ourselves from everyone else, is our unique pattern of hopes, fears, and desires.

Where do our hopes, fears, and desires reside? In our imagination. Imagination, I have said, is our access to the past and to the future, taking us beyond present awareness. Other creatures have awareness but not imagination (which requires consciousness); therefore, they can have no hopes, fears, and desires. Their hopes are mere drives to find food, safety, and a mate. Their desires are brute instincts. And they can have no fear, only dread.

HUMAN HOPES

I won't even attempt to catalog what the range or limits of human hopes might be. They can't be summed up as the pursuit of happiness, though that is frequently cited as a prime candidate. People will set aside immediate considerations of happiness, comfort, and well-being to work toward some external consideration (like the well-being of others), now or in the future.

I'd be more inclined to say that satisfaction, fulfillment, arises in the pursuit of our own objectives, in our efforts to be constructive in the world—in the absence of insurmountable frustration or despair. But that could just be a personal difference.

Without hope we are barely human, but with hope the possibilities are unlimited.

The same applies to our fears and desires—they are uncountable. They spring from the imagination and are all based on the way we see ourselves.

We don't expect others to share all our hopes, fears, and desires. That is what makes them different from us and enables us to see ourselves as different from them.

It is through our feelings, our consciousness, and our hopes, fears, and desires that we identify ourselves and everyone else as individuals.

It is through feelings, consciousness, hopes, fears, and desires, and the recognition of our powers and limitations that we stop being merely *Us,* and become *Ourselves.*

Selected References

Ahn, Woo-Kyoung, Robert L. Goldstone, Bradley C. Love, Arthur B. Markman, and Phillip Wolff (2005). *Categorization Inside and Outside the Laboratory.* Washington, DC: American Psychological Association.

Birtchnell, John (2003). *The Two of Me: The Rational Outer Me and the Emotional Inner Me.* New York: Routledge.

Damasio, Antonio (1999). *The Feeling of What Happens: Body and Emotion in the Making of Consciousness.* New York: Harcourt.

Dodwell, Peter (2000). *Brave New Mind: A Thoughtful Inquiry Into the Nature and Meaning of Mental Life.* New York: Oxford University Press.

Donald, Merlin (2001). *A Mind So Rare. The Evolution of Human Consciousness.* New York: Norton.

Gold, Paul E. and William T. Greenough (Eds.) (2001). *Memory Consolidation.* Washington, DC: American Psychological Association.

Pinker, Steven (2002). *The Blank Slate: The Modern Denial of Human Nature.* New York: Viking.

Praetorius, Nini (2000). *Principles of Cognition, Language and Action.* Dordrecht, Netherlands: Kluwer.

Saul, John Ralston (1992). *Voltaire's Bastards.* Toronto, Canada: Penguin.

Smith, Frank (1990). *to think.* New York: Teachers College Press.

Smith, Frank (1998). *The Book of Learning and Forgetting.* New York: Teachers College Press.

Sternberg, Robert J. (1999). *The Nature of Cognition.* Cambridge, MA: MIT Press.

Tulving, Endel and Fergus I. M. Craik (2000). *The Oxford Handbook of Memory.* New York: Oxford University Press.

Wright, Ronald (2004). *A Short History of Progress.* Toronto, Canada: Anansi.

Index